Policy Analysis in
Political Science

The Nelson-Hall Series in Political Science

Consulting Editor: *Samuel C. Patterson*
University of Iowa

Randall B. Ripley

Policy Analysis in Political Science

Nelson-Hall Publishers *nh* Chicago

Library of Congress Cataloging in Publication Data

Ripley, Randall B.
  Policy analysis in political science.

  Bibliography: p.
  Includes index.
  1. Political science. 2. Policy sciences.
3. Political planning—United States. 4. United States—
Politics and gevernment. I. Title.
JA74.R54 1985   350.007′2   84-22607
ISBN 0-8304-1058-9

Manufactured in the United States of America

10 9 8 7 6 5 4 3 2 1

The paper in this book is pH neutral (acid-free).

Contents

List of Tables

List of Figures

Preface

A focus on public policy has become fashionable in political science in the United States in the last few years. In a profound sense, those who have taken politics seriously through the centuries have done so in large part because they took policy and the public welfare seriously. Plato, Aristotle, Aquinas, Machiavelli, Hobbes, Locke, Rousseau, Marx, and their colleagues in twenty-five centuries of investigation of and speculation about political matters were also investigating and speculating about matters of public policy. But in the mid and late twentieth century in the United States, contemporary political scientists did not move easily between broad theoretical notions (often normative in whole or in part), investigations of political phenomena, and investigations of policy phenomena. Most practicing political scientists seemed to view the three enterprises as quite separate. Thus, theorists did their thing; students of political phenomena did their thing—and split the world into various functional and geographical areas because it was much too large and complex to swallow whole; and students of public policy set out to do their thing, for the most part convinced that it was "new" and quite different from either the broad theoretical tradition or the tradition of empirically based analytic knowledge of politics.

As the public policy crowd became self-conscious and then grew in size (modern self-consciousness in the United States probably was given its most important boost after World War II by Daniel Lerner and Harold Lasswell in their edited 1951 book, *The Policy Sciences: Recent Developments in Scope and Methods*), inevitably certain disagreements emerged. Or, perhaps more to the point, no agreement was sought or deemed necessary on certain matters. Perhaps one of the most interesting disagreements was whether the study and, ultimately, evaluation of policy required a new discipline (policy science), an amalgam of subfields of existing disciplines ("the policy sciences" in Lasswell's phrase), or simply augmented subfields in one or more disciplines, including political science.

Without necessarily showing much thought or self-awareness on the point, some practitioners of policy analysis often proceeded to reunite the three traditions mentioned above, although they did so in a variety of ways and with differing emphases. Normative theoretical concerns, empirical concerns with the major features of political systems, and concerns focused on the content of policies and programs themselves all appeared in a variety of work loosely called policy analysis or policy studies.

The present volume is based on the assumption that, ultimately, many disciplines can and must contribute to policy analysis in its fullest sense. A number of social sciences are central to developing policy analysis, and in any given substantive area some scientific and engineering disciplines may also be central. This volume also proceeds on the basis of a belief that, before political scientists forego their own particular focus and leap into some multidisciplinary enterprise (up to and including a new "policy science"), they should perfect their own contributions to the study of policy within the framework of their own discipline.

I recognize that a focus on policy is evolving in a number of academic disciplines, including political science, but cross-disciplinary discussion is quite limited. On some points of discussion there is at least a rudimentary form of agreement among political scientists. On other points there is no agreement evident. There is considerable ferment and often some interesting debate. I accept the unstable, partially formulated state of a policy focus in political science as both natural and desirable at this stage of its development. I will make some assertions in the book about various aspects of policy studies, but the reader should recognize that these assertions are tentative and sometimes hypothetical. As the policy focus continues to emerge and develop, I am quite willing to change my mind, both about things I know I am not sure about and about things I discover I am no longer sure about. Unbending quasi-theological stances about one's own discipline have always seemed silly to me, and they seem even more pointless when the endeavor is new and developing.

This volume has two main themes, which are interwoven throughout the various chapters. One theme addresses the question of how to think about or conceptualize the policy process in the United States. The second theme addresses various aspects of how to think about policy analysis itself—its nature, its real and potential contributions, its real and potential limitations—and the relationship of political scientists and other social scientists to actors in the world of policy and programs.

This is not a book on how to do policy analysis, nor is it a book specifying techniques for the analysis of policy. It is largely a conceptual book, buttressed by some examples drawn from empirical analysis. It is also an argumentative book, although the arguments are not offered in the belief that they are final truth. It is a book by a political scientist, grounded in political science, and based on the belief that political scientists should put in order their own thinking about what they can and cannot contribute to policy analysis before seeking to join a broader social science policy analytic enterprise.

The book is focused on policy analysis in the United

States, primarily at the national level. The first three chapters address a number of general concerns. Chapter one focuses on various aspects of the relationship between political science and public policy, chapter two offers an overview of the nature of the policy process, and chapter three discusses the notion of types of policy responses. The next three chapters explore in more detail major clusters of policy activity that have served as foci for different policy analytic efforts: chapter four assesses the study of agenda building, formulation, and legitimation; chapter five deals with the nature and evaluation of implementation; and chapter six comments on the nature and evaluation of impact. Chapter seven concludes the book with some thoughts on the nature of the policy analytic task.

My thanks to three colleagues who read the entire manuscript and offered helpful comments: Grace A. Franklin of Ohio State University, Charles O. Jones of the University of Virginia, and Samuel C. Patterson of the University of Iowa. Franklin also did the basic research on the short cases reported at the ends of chapters 4 and 5. Lance deHaven-Smith of Florida Atlantic University read some parts of the manuscript and provided useful reactions. A number of the ideas that are developed in the book were refined in discussion with a large number of able Ohio State students who have taken my courses on various aspects of policy analysis and the policy process over the years. A number of the professionals at Nelson-Hall have made the process of production relatively painless, at least for me. Edith Bivona made the word processor at the Mershon Center at Ohio State do wonderful things rapidly in preparing the manuscript. As has been the case for a number of years, I am grateful to the Mershon Center (directed by Charles F. Hermann) for its vital support for a broad range of my endeavors, including this one.

1
Political Science and Public Policy

There are those who view policy analysis as an enterprise basically different in character from the policy-related intellectual activity in any relevant discipline, including political science. For them, the title of this book, *Policy Analysis in Political Science*, would make little sense, since they would deny that policy analysis in their conception could be located, even in part (which is all I propose), in any traditional discipline.

One of the best statements of this point of view is made by Brewer and deLeon (1983). They define social sciences as sciences and then contrast the problems faced by scientists with the problems faced by policy analysts: "All sciences seek the development of theory by the generation and testing of hypotheses that confirm, refine, and enlarge common understandings of events. . . . A well-developed scientific discipline permits small bits of fresh information, in combination with its laws and theories, to generate valid predictions of wide scope. But science's success is owed in part to the care its practitioners take in selecting their problems. It also results from the consistency of the client for the work: the discipline itself, as repre-sented by its adherents.

1

"For practical problems that demand policy responses, the scientific procedures are not applicable. . . .

"The policy sciences and policy analysts try . . . to provide suggestions and guidance for courses of action to persons in authority or with power to change circumstances. Policy analysis is therefore severely disadvantaged compared to conventional science by its inability to choose its own problems, by the complexity of the problems it confronts, and by the limited scope and power of the tools at its disposal" (p. 3).

Brewer and deLeon conclude their discussion of policy analysis versus disciplinary science by making the divorce complete: "Policy sciences is not a simple, incremental modification of any of the standard disciplinary or professional approaches. It is a fundamental change in outlook, orientation, methods, procedures, and attitude. This is not to say that the traditional disciplines are not valuable or have nothing to contribute; we have already pointed out their importance. It is to say that the challenge of doing policy analysis well is not equivalent to doing disciplinary work well. They are different enterprises with distinctive approaches and objectives" (p. 6).

An earlier statement by sociologist James S. Coleman (1972) equates "policy research" with "the study of the impact of public policy as an aid to future policy" and likewise concludes that disciplinary research and policy research are two very different enterprises. Policy analysis (or policy research) is, in this view, a new and different enterprise.

A very different view is held by those who see policy studies as very broad and thoroughly interwoven with many disciplines, especially as an effort in political science. A good statement of this position was made by Dennis Palumbo, writing an introduction to the first volume of a new journal, *Policy Studies Review* (1981:6): "Policy studies is similar to political theory in at least the following respect: it is part of every field of political science. For example, legislative politics is relevant to policy studies because it is important to policy formation; research in public administration is relevant to policy studies because implementation, which is an important aspect of policy studies, is what public administration is all about; and all fields of political science do some research in substantive policy areas such as crime, welfare, education, housing, planning, health, environment, and energy.

"In this sense it is true that political science always has been involved in policy studies research in that the discipline has helped us understand various aspects of the policy cycle. But current policy studies research isn't just a continuation of traditional political science in a new garb, for it has added new concepts and dimensions to our understanding of the policy cycle."

Palumbo then broadens policy studies beyond political science and makes the broadest possible claim for it: "The fact is that policy studies is no longer the sole domain of political science. Policy studies has been defined in many ways. We will define it broadly here to refer to any research that relates to or promotes the public interest" (p. 8).

There are numerous other positions on the nature of policy analysis, policy research, and policy studies (none of the phrases has a fixed and widely accepted meaning), and on the relationship of any of them to a variety of disciplines, principally those in the social sciences and principally political science within the social science subset. What are we to make of the quoted views? And, most important, where do I start this volume in terms of the position on the relationship between public policy and political science in a broad sense?

First, I reject the definition offered by Palumbo as too broad to define any limits at all. The term "public interest" has no particular meaning except that given to it by any given individual. Policy studies as defined by Palumbo—no doubt for good practical reasons in trying to get a new journal off the ground with interesting, high-quality contributions—leaves most of political science, and most of many other disciplines in the social sciences, indistinguishable from policy studies. Palumbo certainly states a descriptive truth when he asserts that much work in political science is preoccupied, at least rhetorically, with policy phenomena. Whether that makes them policy studies in some definable sense is quite another matter. As used by Palumbo, policy studies encompasses whatever any author claims is related to policy. That position is all right except that it leaves very little basis on which to judge the relevance of any given piece of work or the advance of the speciality of policy studies as a whole.

Nor am I satisfied by the insistence of Brewer and deLeon that policy analysis is separate from existing disciplines and is, in fact, an identifiable enterprise characterized by "a fundamental change in outlook, orientation, methods, procedures, and attitude" when compared to any "standard disciplinary or professional approaches." There may be such policy analysis, and it may be exemplified best in the work done in a variety of policy research organizations, both for-profit and nonprofit. As stipulated by Brewer and deLeon and Coleman, this work has only marginal ties to what they would call disciplinary research. Mutual isolation of policy analysis from disciplinary analysis is reinforced to the extent that those doing disciplinary analysis would tend to be located in universities and those doing policy analysis would tend to be located outside universities.

I take the position that political science has a great deal to contribute to the study of policy, indeed to policy analysis. I use the phrase "policy analysis" not in the rather grandiose sense in which Brewer and deLeon use it but in a more restricted sense—one tied specifically to political science, at least at this stage of the development of the systematic attention to policy and of the discipline of political science itself. I do not rule out the notion that ultimately the concept of "policy analysis in political science" (the title of this volume) may become outmoded, because policy analysis will necessarily partake of skills and will address topics that require that the persons involved not be political sci-

Figure 1.1

The Spectrum of Policy Studies and Policy Analysis

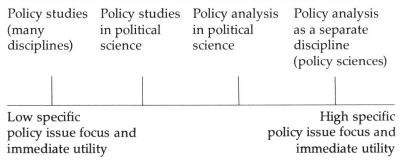

Policy studies (many disciplines)	Policy studies in political science	Policy analysis in political science	Policy analysis as a separate discipline (policy sciences)

Low specific policy issue focus and immediate utility

High specific policy issue focus and immediate utility

entists (or members of any other single discipline). However, that development, if it ever occurs, seems to me to be in the distant future. At present and for the foreseeable future, the notion of policy analysis of a peculiarly political science stripe seems both possible and desirable. I certainly do not make the foolish claim that only political scientists can be policy analysts. What I do claim is that political scientists, *among others,* can be good policy analysts precisely because they can enrich their analysis with the insights, theories, and techniques of their home discipline.

This discussion of the different ways of conceiving of systematic work on policy phenomena can be summarized visually in at least two ways. Figure 1.1 shows a spectrum that runs from low specific focus on policy issues coupled with low immediate utility as a goal of the work at one end to high specific focus on specific policy issues coupled with high immediate utility as a goal of the work at the other end. Four points have been entered on the spectrum. This is drawn as a spectrum, however, because the four points are not thoroughly formulated positions, that is, each of the illustrative points still has some fuzziness about it, and any two definers (or even advocates) of any of the positions would be likely to disagree on some important defining characteristics. It is important to realize that in the empty spaces of the spectrum other positions that have combinations of views and characteristics are possible, and some of these positions have, no doubt, been espoused and articulated.

Four positions have been identified:

1. *Policy studies* coming from a variety of disciplines is loosely defined. It is not grounded in any single discipline nor does it pretend to generate a new discipline. It does not necessarily focus on specific substantive policy issues and does not intend to be immediately useful to policy makers, policy implementers, or other policy actors.

2. *Policy studies in political science* is, by definition, intertwined with political science. Only sometimes does it focus on specific substantive policy issues, and only sometimes does it intend to be immediately useful to any of a variety of policy actors.

3. *Policy analysis in political science* is a part of political science, aims at focusing on specific policy issues much of the time, and is concerned with a relatively high degree of immediate utility to some subset of policy actors.

4. *Policy sciences* (policy analysis as a separate discipline) is, by definition, a new discipline related tangentially to a variety of disciplines. It is concerned only with specific (current) policy issues and is dedicated to a high degree of immediate utility for various subsets of policy actors.

Another way of considering the differences between these four illustrative points of view is presented in the 2 x 2 matrix in figure 1.2. One dimension is the relative degree of grounding in and interaction with political science. The other dimension is the degree of focus on substantive policy issues. The two forms of policy analysis have a relatively high degree of focus on substantive policy issues but differ

Figure 1.2

Types of Policy Analysis

		Degree of Substantive Policy Issue Focus	
		High	Low
Degree of Grounding in and Interaction with Political Science	High	Policy analysis in political science	Policy studies in political science
	Low	Policy sciences (policy analysis as a separate discipline)	Policy studies (many disciplines)

in their degree of grounding in and interaction with political science. The two forms of policy studies have a relatively low degree of focus on substantive policy issues but differ in their degree of grounding in and interaction with political science. This book will deal with policy analysis in political science not as the only viable way for political scientists to study policy profitably but as one possible way (with both strengths and weaknesses).

I will return to some specifications of the area of policy analysis within political science after I discuss briefly some of the general features of good political science and some of the shifting attitudes in the discipline toward how to do productive work and what role policy can and should play in that work. Following those discussions I will turn to the roles and contributions of political scientists in policy analysis and the relationships between various kinds of scholarly actors and policy actors.

Attributes of Productive Political Science

As I ponder the history of political science, I come to the conclusion that the most productive work has certain characteristics. Likewise, as I ponder policy analysis done by political scientists I find the same characteristics present. Thus, I would argue that the marks of productive political science are also the marks of good policy analysis done by political scientists.

I hasten to add that in no way do I view policy analysis as somehow "superior" to other forms of political science. Political science is by nature a diverse discipline. There will be and should be lots of enterprises going on all of the time under the rubric of political science. I think that policy analysis as conceived in the present volume should be one of them. More specifically, I think it is both valid and desirable for some political scientists to want to do research on topics that are part of the current policy agenda in the United States (or any country or the international arena) and to want to disseminate the results of their research to relevant policy makers. This does not mean that all political scientists should be engaged in such activities, but that the diversity of the discipline has room for systematic work of this character. Society has something to gain from this work.

What characterizes the most productive political science, including policy analysis in political science? First, theorizing is essential to any productive enterprise. If the word *theory* is too threatening, then the same point can be made by insisting on the indispensability of conceptualizing or model building in any serious political science inquiry. These theories, models, and concepts can be derived and employed both deductively and inductively (probably a mix is desirable). But the kinds of generalizations and specifications required by the theoretical enterprise are vital. Without this kind of abstract guidance, individual studies become masses of detail with no clear map to show why those details are important, and, worse yet, the studies never cumulate.

Second, good political science, including its policy analysis component, must be empirically oriented. This is another way of saying that theorizing for its own sake turns out to be lifeless unless some of the propositions contained in or derived from the theories are tested with empirical data. Thus, for me, political science (including the focus on policy variables) involves data, hypothesis formulation, hypothesis testing, and other formal attributes of a systematic empirical enterprise.

Perhaps the most important set of characteristics denoting productive political science is what I would call the scientific aspiration. "Good science" is achievable in political science endeavors, including those involving policy analysis. This does not mean that there is a set form for all "good science" or that every research project will look the same in design and methodology. There are at least five central features to "good science" or, to use the phrase I prefer, to the "scientific aspiration" in political science.

1. The question of cause-and-effect is central no matter what the specific subject matter is. Political science—and the policy analysis subset of political science efforts—must always pose the question, Why? It must always seek explanations. Phenomenon X (the dependent behavior observed) needs to be explained in terms of phenomena A, B, C, etc. (the independent and intervening behaviors observed).

2. All phenomena and their interrelationships need constantly to be analyzed to see what patterns are present, and those patterns need to be pushed into more abstract levels that encompass increasingly large subsets of behavior. No one has put this point better than Rosenau (1968:204) "Stated most succinctly, a scientific consciousness involves an automatic tendency to ask, 'Of what larger pattern is this behavior an instance?' " Pushing toward abstraction and looking for more encompassing patterns also means that comparative analysis is essential. In order

to see if patterns exist, relationship "A leads to B" must be compared to relationship "X leads to Y" to see if they have something in common. The typical frames of comparison of phenomena in political science, including policy analysis, involve one or more of the following: across time, across different processes, across different substantive areas, or across different geographical areas (within single nations or between nations).

3. A reasonable goal to pursue is to seek regularities among causal relationships and patterns of those relationships that are so strong that they allow the prediction of results in similar cases in the abstract. These predictions can then be tested by future events. In the case of policy analysis, they are tested in an action setting. Some independent or intervening variables can be deliberately changed or manipulated to foster desired outcomes.

4. Empirical research should be conducted so that replication (that is, repeating the procedures on different data and/or repeating the procedures on the same data) can be done. Such replication should be done using additional or different data dealing with the relationship(s) originally examined. This leads either to discarding findings or to developing greater confidence in them. Naturally, if replication is to be possible, careful, systematic records of data sources, procedures, and methods must be kept and made widely accessible.

5. Research should be designed in the belief that knowledge is cumulative. A new piece of work should not start from ground zero or anywhere near ground zero in terms of its theoretical and empirical underpinnings. Rather, the research must accept some matters as true or as proven and make some other (explicit) assumptions. The researcher must place some bets at the outset (during design) of research. Only then can questions of a somewhat more advanced order be asked.

Naturally, some of the beginning bets may turn out to be bad ones. Destructively false assumptions may be used. Mistakes in theories or in empirical realities accepted as true may be discovered too late to save the research in question. Thus, some research, even that which is well designed, may lead down blind allies for one reason or another. But that is preferable to the endless building of theory and empirical tests from scratch each time, where it is evident that author twenty-two either has not read or finds nothing trustworthy in the work of authors one through twenty-one.

Shifting Attitudes Toward the Analysis of Politics and Policy

Modern American political science has undergone a series of rapid shifts in prevailing attitudes toward the legitimacy and/or essentiality of some features of the analytic enterprise in which it is engaged. In part, this is similar to shifts that have occurred just as rapidly in the other social sciences, particularly sociology. "Prevailing attitudes" is an arbitrary construction on the part of the observer (in this case, me). Underlying the notion that some attitudes become "prevailing" is the observation that no attitude is held by all or even nearly all political scientists at any given time. Debates continue over the nature and shape of the discipline and the nature of the most productive work to be done and the most productive ways to do it. Thus, there are always important minority viewpoints that dissent in whole or in part from the "prevailing attitudes" present in the discipline at any given time.

The fact that fashions in opinions about the discipline itself (and the place or lack of place for policy analysis in it) have changed fairly rapidly means that by now there is a fairly heterogeneous set of views represented by different important individuals and groups of individuals calling themselves political scientists. This is in part because a wide range of ages is represented in the discipline, which means that graduate training was acquired not only at different graduate schools and with different professors but also at different points of time. In my own department in early 1984, for example, no one had yet reached the numerical age of sixty, yet the Ph.D.s of department faculty had been awarded over a thirty-year period, between the early 1950s and the early 1980s. That wouldn't make much difference if the discipline had remained stable over that period, but it had changed rapidly. And, of course, people getting a Ph.D. in 1955 may well have studied with people who got their own training thirty or more years earlier than that.

In short, the fact of changing opinion, the differences in age of both trainees and trainers, and the different mixes of opinion in leading graduate departments of political science mean that, at any given time, a variety of opinions are represented even within a seemingly prevailing consensus. Added to this stew of opinions is the fact that political science is a discipline that is derived from a number of roots (history, philosophy, law, political economy, sociology) and that has a number of important ties with other disciplines (psychology, economics, geography, statistics, computer science). People also have very different substantive interests that can all fall under the rubric of political science.

There are five matters on which changing patterns of attitudes are discernible over the last fifty to seventy years of American political science. These matters involve the legitimacy and/or essentiality of specific activities in the analysis of politics, including policy. The five items can be put in question form in either a mythical or real debriefing of any political scientist in terms of core values he or she holds:

1. Is a focus on the substance of public policy legitimate and/or essential in political science at least some of the time?
2. Are normative/prescriptive concerns legitimate and/or essential in political science at least some of the time?

3. Is quantification legitimate and/or essential in many/ most/all empirical inquiries about political and policy phenomena?
4. Is methodological rigor legitimate and/or essential in political science inquiries, including those dealing with policy?
5. Is the use of history (or to use the appropriate jargon, longitudinal studies) legitimate and/or essential in studies of policy and politics?

Table 1.1

Attitudes Toward the Analysis of Politics and Policy

Are the following legitimate and/or essential in the analysis of politics and policy?

"School" and "Era"	Substantive Policy Focus	Normative/ Prescriptive Concerns	Quantifi- cation	Methodo- logical Rigor	Use of History
Prebehavioral: Pre-1945	yes	yes	no	no	yes
Behavioral Revolution: 1945–1960	no	no	yes	yes	no
Refined Behavioralism: 1960–1970	no	no	yes	yes	yes
Postbehavioralism: Post-1965	yes	no	yes	yes	yes
The "New Left" Alternative: Post-1965	yes	yes	no	no	yes
The "Policy Analysis and Evaluation" Alternative: Post-1970	yes	yes	yes	yes	yes

At least six different patterns of answers have appeared over the years in the United States (although patterns 1 and 5 contain the same literal answers when they are dichotomized yes and no, the meanings and purposes behind the answers are quite different). Different patterns have also tended to be related to certain periods of time. A brief discussion of these patterns follows. Keep in mind that the attributed time periods are rough guesses about when different patterns of views were at their strongest. Table 1.1 summarizes in simplified fashion the central ideas of the discussion that follows.

The Prebehavioral Era: Pre-1945

American political science in the twentieth century up to the end of World War II was dominated by individuals we have come to think of as prebehavioral. (I ignore the nineteenth century roots of twentieth century American political science, although they are interesting, because they are not directly relevant to the argument I am making here. On some of the early developments see Crick, 1959, and Somit and Tanenhaus, 1967.) Few people in the discipline today are old enough to have known personally the leading individuals from before 1945. When their work is reviewed today, their answers to our questions are generally quite clear (although they would not be shared by the mavericks of the 1920s or 1930s, including such people as Charles Merriam or Harold Lasswell). They believed in a substantive policy focus and in making prescriptions about "good" organizational and institutional arrangements and about "good" policy. Most had no particular or abiding interest in quantification or in methodological rigor. With some notable exceptions these were not issues that concerned them much, although there are some notable exceptions. They certainly tended to believe in the validity and necessity of using historical information in understanding and prescribing for a current situation.

The Behavioral Revolution: 1945–1960

In the immediate postwar period, the disciples of Merriam and Lasswell and others had made a revolution in the discipline (a revolution paralleled in most of the other social sciences in the United States within a few decades before or after the events in political science). This "behavioral revolution" took root and flourished in its original form in a number (but by no means all) of the strongest graduate departments. Like good revolutionaries everywhere the leaders of this particular revolution rejected all of the values of those against whom they felt themselves to be rebelling. Therefore, they rejected a focus on both substantive policy and on normative or prescriptive concerns, in part because they felt the two went hand-in-hand. That is, if one focused on substantive policy issues, prescription seemed inevitable. Both were rejected.

The original revolutionists were concerned with the necessity of quantification. They also expressed adherence to the importance of methodological rigor. In retrospect, it seems as if they assumed that if one quantified, the canons of methodological rigor were satisfied, and that if one did not quantify, it was impossible to be rigorous. Finally, the revolutionaries rejected the use of history (or longitudinal studies). This produced some odd results, such as occurred when a fine book by Matthews (1960) on the U.S. Senate analyzed quite well and interestingly a particular period— the late 1940s and most of the 1950s—but was treated as an analysis of how the Senate always had worked and always would work.

The behavioral revolution has shaped much of post-World War II political science in the United States in a variety of ways. A number of refinements and specific disagreements with some revolutionary premises and beliefs have emerged, but most political scientists practicing the trade today are in agreement, perhaps without realizing it, with some of the basic points made by the revolutionists— particularly their stress on quantification and (after refinements) on methodological rigor. Only the "new left" alternative, discussed below, rejects all of the five principal values of the revolutionists outlined above.

Refined Behavioralism: 1960–1970

During this period, the only answer to the five central questions that was changed in flat terms by the initial refiners of behavioralism was to readmit the utility, legitimacy, and necessity of the study of history (or, to put it another way, "longitudinal" studies rather than simply "cross-sectional" studies—those that focused on a single point in time or a short period of clustered points in time). Another important refinement not apparent in table 1.1 was that this set of scholars began to articulate the difference between quantification and methodological rigor. They believed in the necessity of both but also realized that they were separable: a study with lots of numbers could also be methodologically sloppy, and studies without a whole lot of numbers could be quite systematic and rigorous.

Postbehavioralism: Post-1965

The major shift in view articulated by the postbehavioralists (probably still the most numerous part of the publishing subset of academic political scientists in the mid-1980s) when compared to the refined behavioralists is that they agreed that a focus on the substance of policy was at least legitimate and in some cases essential to the analytical thrust of political science. However, most of them continued to reject the legitimacy, let alone the essentiality, of taking normative positions or making prescriptions. Most (although not all) of the contributors to the landmark book edited by Ranney in 1968, *Political Science and Public Policy*, take these two views. Postbehavioralists continue to insist on appropriate quantification and on methodological rigor regardless of the degree of quantification. They also accept the essentiality of longitu-dinal data.

The "New Left" Alternative: Post-1965

In the mid- and late-1960s, a group of political scientists in colleges and universities began to object to two major sets of events and beliefs and actions. First, they were repelled by the military involvement of the United States in Southeast Asia. Second, and simultaneously, they rejected the ruling paradigm, as they saw it, of American political science. The often acrimonious debates that took place throughout the discipline in individual departments and at professional meetings of regional and national political science associa-tions (particularly the American Political Science Associa-tion) mixed the two issues into one odd melange of disagree-ments. Since the end of the Vietnamese war, the acrimony has lessened, but the "new left" (or Caucus for a New Politi-cal Science) has continued to mix political issues and ques-tions about the nature of political science.

The pattern of values held by the "new left" approxi-mates, but for quite different purposes, those held by the prebehavioral political scientists. Above all, the new left is interested in substantive policy and in making prescriptions about that policy. They are not much interested in quantifi-cation or methodological rigor. And they are quite anxious to use history selectively and argumentatively to buttress their policy positions.

The "Policy Analysis and Evaluation" Alternative: Post-1970

A moderately sizeable group of political scientists in the 1970s and 1980s offered another slight variation on the basic values in their answers to the five questions. Basically, they are distinguished from the postbehavioralists on only one ground: they are concerned with reaching normatively based on conclusions and making prescriptions as well as doing solid empirical work based on longitudinal data, appropriate quantification, and methodological rigor. In short, they seek to stress the systematic, rigorous aspects of political science, including political science used to analyze policy. But they deny that a concern with prescription is prohibited by a concern with rigor or "science." They find the two enterprises compatible, although they understand the differences between them.

The "Subfield" of Policy Analysis

In the introductory pages of this chapter, I wrestled briefly with the various meanings of policy analysis and policy studies. No doubt a whole book could be written on these distinctions, but the purpose of this book would not be served by such lengthy discussions. Rather, I want to describe the concerns of the "subfield" of policy analysis in political science and then go on to the nature of the policy process and policy making and to the role of the political scientist in relation to policy actors. In this spirit, then, the following working definition of the policy analysis subfield in political science is offered:

The policy analysis subfield in political science focuses on (1) the processes of decision making about matters perceived to be in the public domain, (2) the contexts of those decisions, and (3) the results of those decisions. The processes include agenda building, formulation, and legitimation. The results include both implementation activities and a variety of impacts on society and specific populations in society. Policy can be treated as a dependent variable (the outcome of decision processes) and as an independent variable (the "intervention" or "treatment" leading to the results that are studied and/or generating the decision processes themselves). Empirical studies include both systematic description and systematic explanation of various policy-related phenomena. Many studies lead to prescriptive conclusions as well as to "scientific" conclusions. Studies may focus on subnational policies, national policies, cross-national comparisons of policies, or policies affecting international and transnational relations.

The Role and Contributions of Political Scientists in Policy Analysis

General Roles for Trained Political Scientists

Trained political scientists can and do play a variety of different roles in their careers. Sometimes they are played serially, or sometimes several may be assumed simultaneously. A few individuals, no doubt, choose one role for themselves and perform only it for an entire career.

What self-images do political scientists have as they consider the question of how their professional life relates to questions of public policy? What major roles can they choose from (the choice is not limited to one role over time or even at any single point in time)? Five roles define the central possibilities: (1) irrelevant scholar; (2) relevant scholar; (3) consulting scholar; (4) official; and (5) citizen.

The Scholarly Roles. The first three roles have to do with how a trained political scientist views his or her contributions as a scholar in relation to questions of public policy. In the first role, "irrelevant scholar," the individual sees his or her first and only responsibility as being to the discipline. Problems for study are chosen on the basis of "scientific" criteria (What gaps are presented by the literature? What are the next logical steps in developing cumulative knowledge about some political phenomena?). No doubt these criteria are tempered by personal taste and personal judgments about what problems have some interest. The "irrelevance" in this role comes about because the scholar does not pay any attention at all to the policy importance or nonimportance of topics chosen. Some topics may, of course, turn out to be relevant or important in a policy sense, but that is not why they are chosen. And, even if the topic has immediate policy interest and relevance, the scholar makes no attempt to relate findings to policy concerns. The findings are related only to disciplinary concerns. The scholar perceives himself or herself to have nothing to say to policy actors. If the policy actors want to mine the scholarly literature for material, that is viewed as their decision and their concern. But the irrelevant scholar will give them no aid, either explicit or implicit.

The above description is meant to be only factual, not judgmental. Most political scientists who do research view themselves as irrelevant scholars when it comes to the choice of what they study and to the dissemination of what they find out. They do not view it as appropriate to choose topics for research because they are related to policy concerns and to disseminate results in special ways and with special efforts for policy actors.

"Irrelevant" scholars can, of course, do superb work, or they can do miserable work, or their work can fall anywhere on the scale between superb and miserable. The point here is simply that policy relevance is not a criterion that interests them or that they think is appropriate at any point in the scholarly process.

The second scholarly role is that of the "relevant scholar." This scholar proceeds as does the irrelevant scholar with the exception that at least some of the time a research topic is chosen in part because it is of some immediate policy importance. This kind of scholar thinks it appropriate (and, presumably, interesting) to frame some research questions because they are related to societal policy concerns. That, however, is not the only criterion he or she uses in choosing topics. This kind of scholar does not feel it incumbent on him or her to make special efforts to disseminate results to policy actors. The quality of work, of course, can again vary from superb to miserable. And, although the intent is to deal with relevant policy topics the resulting analysis may turn out to be largely irrelevant.

The third scholarly role is that of the "consulting scholar." This individual is like the relevant scholar in that he or she chooses topics, at least some of the time, because of their policy relevance. He or she is "consulting" in the sense that the results of policy-relevant studies are explicitly offered to policy actors because they are thought to have some interest in them. The offering of the results may also involve the use of different formats for presentation of findings, ranging from special policy-oriented papers and memos to verbal briefings for bureaucrats or legislative staff or formal testimony for legislative committees. Naturally, the quality of the work done by this subset of scholars also varies a great deal.

The Nonscholarly Roles. Two additional roles open to political scientists are separate from (although they may be mixed with) the three possible scholarly roles. The first of these is the role of "official." Some trained political scientists choose to become an appointed governmental official (and occasionally even an elected official). Such a role can be played simultaneously with any of the scholarly roles if the job is part-time (as with jobs such as member of the city council, member of the local school board, county commissioner, member of an appointed executive branch commission or task force, or members of many state legislatures). If the job is full-time (for example, as a full-time employee of federal, state, or local government or as a member of some state legislatures or Congress, or as a paid lobbyist), then time simply is not available to play a scholarly role, and the "official" role becomes dominant.

The second nonscholarly role is that of citizen. Political scientists are obviously free to accept or reject various levels of citizen responsibility that inevitably relate to current policy issues. Some reject the role of citizen altogether. More accept some part of it but limit their activities. A few are active citizens and participate aggressively in political campaigns, public hearings, and so on. These choices are up to individuals, and specific choices about degree of citizen involvement are compatible, in principle, with any of the three scholarly roles.

Potential Contributions of Political Scientists to Different Policy Activities

There are many ways of cutting up the policy process analytically in terms of describing both political processes that take place and attendant intellectual processes. The political and intellectual processes blend. It is not my purpose here to enumerate or to analyze the various ways of conceiving of the political or the intellectual processes. I will turn in more detail in chapter 2 to the nature of the policy process. At present I simply want to stipulate a reasonable definition of policy activities (chronological in form, although I offer them with the full realization that the chronology presented is often scrambled) for purposes of commenting on possible contributions and the limits on those contributions on the part of political scientists at each stage or in each activity.

The six sets of activities (which can be analyzed both in terms of political processes and an intellectual dimension) are:

1. agenda setting
2. goal setting
3. alternative development and selection
4. implementation of the selected alternative
5. evaluation of implementation
6. evaluation of results (impact)

Comments follow on the potential contributions of "consulting scholars" who are political scientists to each of the six stages. Each discussion begins with a brief indication of the nature of the stage itself.

Agenda Setting. The agenda setting stage refers to the processes—both political and intellectual—by which problems get selected for governmental action. In principle there are many problems "out there" to which government can pay attention. But, in fact, only a subset—even though large—is on the governmental agenda at any given time. What contribution are political scientists who view themselves as "consulting scholars" likely to be able to make to agenda setting?

In general, the impact is slight. It tends to develop in one of two ways. Good political science will get transformed into a form that can have an impact on agenda setting either by accident or through the "translation" of a popular writer. Individual scholars that set out deliberately to have their work taken seriously and have an impact on agenda setting are fated to be frustrated most of the time.

Groups of scholars that include political scientists and that are organized into some sort of "institute" concerned in part with agenda building may well focus the work of those scholars so as to have such an impact. The work of scholars located in such settings as the Brookings Institution and the American Enterprise Institute (AEI) provide good examples. Likewise, some clusters of scholars that often include political scientists, who focus on specific areas of the world outside the United States, may have the chance of affecting the agenda of the United States with respect to those areas or a specific nation within an area. The chances for impact are probably enhanced if a country that is the subject of focus is relatively small and unknown in the United States. In short, political scientists are not likely to play a major role as consulting scholars in the agenda setting process. Much broader forces tend to shape the agenda. I will return to the theme of studying agenda setting in chapter 4.

Goal Setting. The goal setting stage refers to the political and intellectual processes by which items on the governmental agenda are considered in some rough sense and one or more goals or broad aims are attached to each item. These goals are likely to be quite vague, and there may also be competing or logically inconsistent goals.

Broad social and political forces are at work as the polity edges toward setting goals for itself on its current agenda items. Individual political scientists may participate in the debates about goals as citizens, but as consulting scholars they almost never have much impact, even if they try. Again, institutions such as Brookings or AEI may provide a partial exception. This stage, then, is not one in which political scientists should spend much time if they hope to have impact on aspects of policy.

Alternative Development and Selection. Once broad goals are arrived at, governmental agencies (both legislative and executive) can begin searching for ways to achieve these goals. This involves the development of different alternatives in the form of general approaches to the problem, specific program designs, and administrative structures. At this stage political scientists have some potential contribution to make. In some cases they should be able to project, based on past research, the likely outcome of choosing different alternatives. These projections can also help influence the basic choices that are made.

This area, then, is one in which labors by political scientists interested in some specific impact on current policy may be worthwhile. We will look at the processes of formulation and legitimation in some more detail in chapter 4. Alternative development and selection are integral parts of those broader processes.

Implementation of the Selected Alternative. Once an alternative has been selected and the word made flesh through the establishment of some kind of program (usually by statute), many concrete activities have to take place in order to implement the good words of the statute (presumably pursuing some of the general goals that turned out to be politically attractive enough to achieve relatively broad support). The job of implementation is primarily that of bureaucrats (at various territorial levels in the case of most domestic policies in the United States). Political scientists who have studied and evaluated implementation (see the next stage) may have meaningful knowledge to offer to the implementers, but as scholars they do not have a direct role to play in implementation.

Evaluation of Implementation. The evaluation of implementation is a relatively new intellectual activity. As always, there are also political elements to evaluation. In this volume "evaluation" does not imply purely "scholarly" processes as opposed to "political" processes. Knowledge is of different orders and intermingles with a variety of factors in a political process. More will be said of that intermingling in chapter 7. Chapter 5 is devoted to a more detailed discussion of the nature and evaluation of implementation.

Political scientists can contribute a great deal to this evaluation. In fact, it is the one activity in which they can be expected to play the lead role. In some ways this may be because those trained in other disciplines do not care much about close analyses of implementation. In other ways it is because implementation is, above all, a political process, and political scientists have better instincts and better training to deal with it systematically than anyone else. In a broad sense political scientists should pursue three major clusters of analytical questions attached to the evaluation of implementation: (1) What actions are taken toward meeting program goals and why? (2) What effects do those actions have on program results and why? (3) What individuals and groups are benefiting at what rate and why?

Evaluation of Results (Impact). Evaluation of results is complicated and tricky. Political scientists can be involved in this form of evaluation, although, unlike evaluation of implementation, they may have fewer skills and even fewer appropriate instincts here than those with training in other social sciences. Clearly, the evaluation of impact must be an interdisciplinary enterprise, with the appropriate mix of training varying depending on what is being evaluated. In chapter 6 I will discuss the evaluation of impact at greater length. Here I simply wish to note that a broad notion of impact should be developed and used and that unintended consequences as well as intended consequences must be studied.

Relations Between Scholars and Policy Actors

Many nuances exist in the various relations between policy scholars and policy actors, and a great deal of ink has been expended writing about these details. The purpose of this section is not to recapitulate what has been said nor to explore all of the important aspects of the relationship. Rather, it is to offer some general thoughts about the relationships as they exist. (More aspects of the relationship will be the subject in chapter 7.)

Four primary groups are involved in the relationship. Two are mainly centered in the scholarly community and two in the "official" community of policy actors, especially in the bureaucracy. The four groups can be roughly characterized as follows:

1. *Policy intellectuals* (see Wilson, 1981, for both a definition of the term and a discussion) are theorists and/or ideologues about broad policy concerns that reside primarily, although not exclusively, in academic institutions. The line between theory and ideology is often blurred, and sometimes the two merge.

2. *Policy researchers*, largely based in academia, are those who do the empirical research on policy.

3. *Policy makers* are those in officialdom (political appointees in the bureaucracy, perhaps a few senior civil servants, and members of Congress at the national level in

the United States) who make policy statements, which are general lines of intention.

4. *Policy bureaucrats* are those in staff positions both in the executive branch (virtually all of them are civil servants) and the legislative branch (some congressional staff members at the national level) who deal with policy—either by doing research, administering research done internally, or administering research done externally on the basis of grants and contracts.

Figure 1.3 summarizes the basis for distinguishing these groups from each other and the closest relationships among these four groups. (Note that the discipline of the policy intellectuals and policy researchers could vary, even though my discussion is focused on political scientists.) One distinction is simply where the individuals happen to be institutionally—typically academia in one case and in the government in the other case. The other distinction has to do with the individuals' degree of empirical orientation, dichotomized as high and low.

Figure 1.3

Relations Between Policy Scholars and Policy Actors

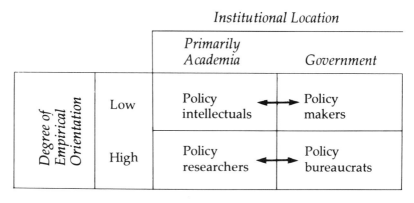

		Institutional Location	
		Primarily Academia	*Government*
Degree of Empirical Orientation	Low	Policy intellectuals ⟷	Policy makers
	High	Policy researchers ⟷	Policy bureaucrats

⟷ = Most prevalent working relationships

As it turns out, the degree of empirical orientation has more force in generating relatively close working relationships than does institutional location. Thus, the policy intellectuals tend to talk with policy makers but also tend to be relatively isolated from their compatriots in academia who do policy research. Likewise, the policy makers tend to be relatively isolated from the policy bureaucrats except as hierarchical necessities during decision making bring them together (these necessities in government are, of course, stronger than in academia, where they may be present but often are not glimpsed let alone seen clearly).

Similarly, policy researchers tend to cultivate relationships with policy bureaucrats and vice versa. In many substantive areas, "research subgovernments" have emerged, in which policy researchers in academic (and some nonacademic) settings and policy bureaucrats in both the executive branch and pieces of Congress, with support from relevant interest groups, see the world in roughly the same terms, at least in relation to what needs to be studied and, perhaps, in relation to what might constitute either "good" or "better" policy.

Some of the literature implies that policy analysis, in any discipline, has minimal impact in large part because folks in and out of government can't get together for a variety of reasons. There are certainly some problems in establishing working relationships and understandings between individuals in government and those outside. At this point I would assert that even larger barriers exist on the basis of how empirically oriented someone is versus how oriented to "broad theory" (even though it is probably not very theoretical in any formal sense). If policy makers work in part on the basis of the grand theoretical alternatives they hear from academia (or from academics who may flit in and out of policy making positions in the executive branch), then policy research, regardless of whether it is done in or out of government and regardless of how interesting it may be to policy bureaucrats, has little or no impact on policy makers.

In political science the problem may be exacerbated because some of the techniques of examining "micro" political behavior through behavioral analysis may not be appropriate to examining and understanding policy (see Lowi, 1973, for this argument, for example). The reader should begin this book well aware that there is no easy and automatic translation of policy analysis into a position of even modest influence in the policy process.

Summary

1. Policy analysis in political science tries to blend a solid grounding in the best of the discipline with a commitment to deal with specific policy issues. This represents a potentially useful focus for scholars interested in policy. This subfield of political science has a broad focus but also has definite boundaries.

2. The characteristics of good policy analysis done by political scientists are the same as the characteristics of good political science in general.

3. Prevailing attitudes in response to a series of key aspects of political science, including the place of policy analysis in the discipline, have changed substantially in the last five to seven decades. Both the discipline and the policy analysis area within it generate continuing debates about the nature of the intellectual and scholarly activity related to policy.

4. Political scientists, in effect, choose some combination of three scholarly and two nonscholarly roles in defining their stance toward involvement with public policy and policy actors. Those who choose to be "consulting scholars" can make their greatest contributions to the development and selection of policy alternatives and to the evaluation of implementation.

5. Individuals both in and out of government with a high degree of empirical orientation in dealing with policy

questions tend to interact frequently. Likewise, those with a low degree of empirical orientation tend to interact frequently. Those in the latter group tend to hold the superior hierarchical positions in the bureaucracy and to be more influential in nongovernmental settings.

2

The Nature of the Policy Process

The policy process is complicated, and the analyst must seek to simplify it. The generic form of simplification used by social scientists, including political scientists, is a model. These models—or simplifications of a very complicated set of processes—can take many different forms, ranging from the purely verbal to the purely mathematical. All of them, however, have the same purpose: to render what is incredibly complex and idiosyncratic in any individual case into a set of relationships that are both simpler and more recurrent. Model makers aim at both understandable patterned description and, sometimes without thinking about it, at explanation (what causes what). This chapter represents my own efforts to "model" in several ways the policy process at the national level in the United States. I will try to make a complicated set of processes understandable in terms of patterns that tend to recur, and I will offer some comments about explanation.

This chapter focuses on models that lay out various stages of policy activity. These models include stages in the policy process that include both political activities and intellectual activities that occur simultaneously (much like the discussion in chapter 1 of the six major policy-related activities and the potential roles of political scientists at each stage). These stages also deal, either implicitly or explicitly, with the policy "products" that emerge over time. And, of course, the ordering of the stages has chronological implications about what might be expected and in what order by anyone looking at the policy process.

A second kind of modeling enterprise starts with the notions that different kinds of policies, differentiated by some broad categorical scheme, are the product of different kinds of political patterns and/or that, when different things are at stake, different kinds of policies help generate different kinds of patterns of political relationships and influence.

Relationships running in both directions (that is, from patterns of interaction to types of policy and from types of policy to patterns of interaction) may be present simultaneously and may reinforce each other. This whole area of exploration will be the subject of chapter 3.

In the rest of this chapter I will look at the utility, limits, and purposes of models in general. Second, I will lay out a simple model for the understanding of policy. Third, I will consider more complicated visions of the U.S. national policy process, and finally, I will summarize in descriptive fashion the flow of policy activities and products of which students of the national policy process in the United States should be aware.

Models: Utility, Purposes, and Limits

Models are not neutral. The choices of what factors seem important to include (and, conversely, what can be excluded) may be shaped, consciously or unconsciously, by ideology or any of a thousand other influences over the mind of the person constructing the model. In short, the general vision of political life is both empirically and theoretically derived. This vision is likely to be included in a model of the policy process.

Utility and Purpose

The major utility of any model is that it simplifies complex reality in ways that can be readily understood. The trick is knowing what level of simplification is appropriate. If a model adheres to too many of the attributes of reality it is seeking to summarize, it becomes unwieldy and too like the original. If, on the other hand, the model becomes too simple and omits too much, it is no longer recognizable enough to be useful in understanding reality.

Modelers of anything face the same general problem. Consider those who want to model railroads. They must choose a scale that allows trains, yards, mainlines, surrounding countryside, and other attributes in and around the real thing to be portrayed sufficiently to give the sense of reality, but with obvious distortions. They must decide what is essential. That usually comes down to preferences for details on cars, especially on locomotives. What is gained in detail is lost in space and vice versa. Ultimately, the scale chosen by any individual modeler becomes a matter of aesthetic taste based, in part, on a judgment of the nature of a satisfactory model. Choices of levels of abstraction and detail in models of political and policy processes partake of the same mix of judgment and aesthetics.

Limits

A specific limit on models of the policy process that needs to be mentioned is that any model (particularly the "flow chart" or "box and arrow" type you will find in this book) is likely to make the world of policy too ordered, too predictable, and too rational. Regardless of the form of the model used, it needs to be realized that:

- The chronology implied in any model of the policy process is only rough at best. Stages may occur "out of order," simultaneously, or in other ways that are not tidy chronologically.
- The boundaries between different stages are blurred and not readily discernible to either participants or analysts in completely clear or consistent ways.

A Simple Model of the Policy Process

As we begin to examine some possible models of the policy process, we must be constantly aware of the purpose of such examinations. Such models are useful in either designing research or in appreciating the studies of others, because they point the reader to the appropriate clusters of variables and to the appropriate relationships between those variables. A model of general applicability and with few variable clusters inevitably points out only the most important variables and the most gross level of relationships to which the observer or researcher must be sensitive. But such a model, although not immediately useful for guiding specific and focused empirical research, is useful in a broader sense because it suggests a general overall vision of the factors that the political science policy analyst must take into account in making sense out of policy phenomena. Thus, we begin with figure 2.1., which portrays the most general model of the policy process.

There are several fairly important ideas embedded in this figure. First, note that the environment and the perceptions of environment on the part of policy actors are partially independent and partially intersecting. Environmental factors can be important even if not perceived by policy actors. Likewise, perceptions—regardless of how accurate or inaccurate they may be—may have independent weight. Analysts define environmental variables in analyzing policy and in trying to figure out what causes certain kinds of policy responses. Some of those analytical constructs have considerable validity, and some of them reveal pressures and forces in society that help explain substantial portions of subsequent policy activity. This is true even if, in some cases, the policy actors themselves are not aware totally, or even aware at all, of the environmental factors that analysts find to be important.

It is also important to note that policy actors move on the basis of their own perceptions. These perceptions include some of the environmental factors that analysts determine to be important. But the perceptions may also be of events, trends, and factors that analysts cannot find systematically important but, in the day-to-day decisions by

Figure 2.1

General Model of the Policy Process

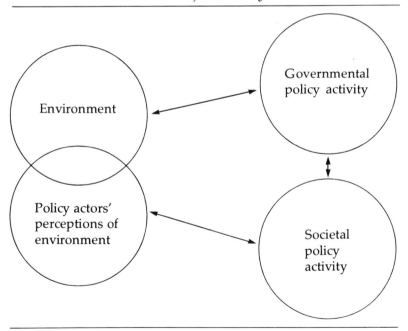

influential actors that shape outcomes in detail, are quite important.

The analyst must pay attention, then, to environmental variables that are uncovered and structured by analytical procedures. But he or she must also pay attention to the perceptions of policy actors as distinct from the analyst's constructs. Actors' perceptions are also "independent variables" that can and usually do have considerable importance in explaining subsequent policy activity.

A second idea that has some importance is that policy activity occurs both in the government and in society. Political scientists interested in policy all too often assume that the activity of government and of governmental actors (members of Congress, presidents, bureaucrats, justices) is all that needs to be studied. To be sure, governmental policy activity is important and requires careful analysis. But equally important is the activity in society that helps shape the general nature of any policy activity. For example, a health clinic may be built by the government, but without the societal activity of individuals choosing to use the clinic nothing much happens. Society and government interact within the context of environment in determining the totality of policy activity. In subsequent discussion I will distinguish between different types of policy activity, but the general point that there are both societal and governmental dimensions to any study of policy should not be missed.

It is worth noting that the arrows, which signify influence or in a rough sense causation, run in both directions between all of the variable clusters. This suggests not just that environment and policy actors' perceptions of the environment "cause" subsequent policy activity in the government and society but that policy activity in both government and society helps shape both the environment and (especially) policy actors' perceptions of it. Likewise, the governmental and societal dimensions of policy activity affect each other.

The notion of "subsequent" policy activity is, in some

ways, misleading. The use of such language suggests that there is a single linear passage of time in which some events take place before some other events and that there are variables that are causative (or independent) and other variables that are resultant (or dependent). Such relationships can be analyzed. In fact, there is no simple linear chronology because all phenomena are constantly present and constantly changing through time, and these changes can have many different chronological relationships to each other. Thus, environment at Time 1 may help "cause" governmental policy activity at Time 2, which may have impact on societal policy activity at Time 3, which in turn may help shape the environment at Time 4, and so on. Even this

Table 2.1

Major Factors for Inclusion in a General Model of the U.S. Policy Process

I.   *Environment*

    A. Outside government
    B. Inside government
    C. Specific policies and programs
    D. Perceptions of policy actors

II. *Governmental Policy Activity*

    A. Policy statements
    B. Policy actions (implementation actions)

III. *Societal Policy Activity*

    A. Societal implementation (usage of programs)
    B. Policy/program results

abstract example is too simple, since it implies that there are predictable cycles of what variables are to be considered independent and dependent at any given time. That may not be altogether true, although the analyst sometimes has to pretend it is true in order to impose some order on an otherwise hopelessly complicated set of relationships.

More Complicated Models of the U.S. Policy Process

Major Factors to Consider

Let's look again at the very simple set of relationships portrayed in figure 2.1. That figure lays out three major clusters of factors (variables) that a policy analyst needs to consider. Those clusters can be elaborated a bit in order to develop a more sophisticated, specific, and practical design for conducting any individual inquiry. Table 2.1 presents an overview of one such elaboration. In the paragraphs that follow I will discuss the major concepts.

Environment: That Outside Government. The first facet of the environment of importance to the policy analyst is the general environment external to government. This signifies that all policy decisions are set in the context of general external environmental factors and that these factors are likely to influence a good deal of what else happens.

The external environment is of two broad types. First, the environment can be described as a series of patterns involving a variety of economic, social, and political factors, including patterns of beliefs and values. These patterns are the constructs of social observers and analysts. For example, unemployment is a genuine feature of the external environment that has the potential for exerting an influence over a good deal else that goes on in the policy process. But the specific form in which unemployment is described—based on a monthly rate broken into population sectors (white males, black teenagers, female heads of household, and so on)—is the construct of social scientists (in this case, economists). Many features of society are in the same mold: they are real, to be sure, but the form of their description is an invention of social scientists. Patterns of portions of the external environment might involve such factors as public opinion, party strength in society, the nature of political coalitions in society, and a great variety of economic and social conditions.

The second type of broad environment is best described as random events. These are not the external constructs of social scientists, even in descriptive form. They are simply events—both natural and those made by people—that occur and have some policy relevance. Major natural disasters (earthquakes, floods, hurricanes, and so on), for example, usually occasion some kind of policy response. Acts of terrorism, national or international, also trigger responses. The analyst needs to acknowledge that such events occur, are generally unpredictable, and have policy consequences that must be analyzed.

Environment: That Inside Government. A second major facet of the environment of importance to the policy analyst is the general internal environment. "Internal" refers to the inside of government in both a structural sense and a process sense. The government has a particular structure and a particular set of operative processes at any given time. These facts have general policy consequences, as do the pattern of relationships between governmental units and nongovernmental interests. Features of the general internal environment that might require systematic attention by an analyst include characteristics of agency structure in the bureaucracy or of subcommittee structure in Congress; characteristics of personnel in agencies or subcommittees; and characteristics of decision-making processes in pieces of the bureaucracy or of Congress.

Environment: That Related to Specific Policies and Programs.   A third major facet of the environment of direct relevance to policy analysis is the specific environment in which any particular policy or program is set. While any individual policy or program is set in the general external and general internal environments described above, any individual policy or program is also set in a context of previous statements and actions. These statements and actions may be in earlier iterations of the policy or program itself, they may be in relation to related forerunner programs, or, at minimum, they describe the context in which the program was formed. No policy or program emerges without some sort of history. If it is an ongoing program or policy, the history is that of the policy or program itself. Even new policies or programs have a prehistory that helps shape the actions, results, and other phenomena at any given time. The notion of incrementalism—that policies and programs tend to change only in small units at any time—is based on the notion, in part, that the specific policy and program environment is a powerful explanatory factor. In short, what occurs in any given time period is a close variant of what existed in the previous time period.

Environment: Perception of Environments by Policy Actors.   All aspects of the environment are subject to some sort of perception (or ignorance) on the part of policy actors. Those perceptions, in a sense, become independent of the phenomena perceived. Thus, both the phenomena and the perceptions can and often do have independent weight in a policy process. The perceptions are most important in helping determine what policy decisions get made. The phenomena—regardless of the accuracy or inaccuracy of perceptions—have the most weight in helping determine what the policies adopted can and cannot accomplish.

Governmental Policy Activity: Policy Statements.   The first major form of governmental policy activity of concern to a policy analyst is the set of activities and processes that result in policy statements. Policy statements are declarations of intent on the part of the government (or a portion of the government) to do something. This declaration is sometimes highly visible, as in a statement by the president or in the passage by Congress of an important new statute. This declaration can also be invisible to most of the public, as in a statement by a bureau chief to an important lobbyist for the bureau's clients. Different levels and different parts of the government may make conflicting policy statements simultaneously. Even the same participant in the policy process may make conflicting statements within a relatively short period of time.

Policy statements may be either intragovernmental or societal in nature. In the former case, they represent an orientation toward the future of specific units of government within the governmental structure. In the latter case, they represent an orientation to what the unit of government will seek to do in society. The latter policy statements are of interest to policy analysts. The former are of primary interest to students of public administration in a more restricted sense.

Governmental Policy Activity: Policy Actions. Policy actions are what the government does as distinguished from what it says it is going to do, sometimes with many and conflicting or unclear voices. Policy actions can also be called implementation actions. Such actions are what happens, typically, after laws are passed authorizing a program, a policy, a benefit, or some kind of tangible governmental output. The set of activities that follow policy statements constitute implementation activities. Implementation activities (to be explored in more detail in chapter 5) include the acquisition of resources needed for action, interpretation of laws (usually through writing regulations), planning for action, organizing action, and providing benefits and services.

Societal Policy Activity: Societal Implementation. Societal implementation refers to patterns of usage or nonusage of programs and intended benefits on the part of those eligible to partake. Or, in a coercive program, such as the draft, societal implementation would refer to such matters as registration rates and evasion rates. In a program conferring benefits—a publicly funded job training program, for example—the rate of usage of training slots for individuals and the nature of the users would both be matters of interest to the policy analyst. Who's involved? Who benefits? It needs to be recognized that not all of those who are eligible may actually show up and take part or benefit in whatever way they are supposed to benefit.

Societal Policy Activity: Policy/Program Results. The results of any policy or program also involve society. The central point of the governing enterprise is—or should be—to have some felicitous impact on society through a variety of policies and programs. The analyst needs to sort out what those impacts or results are and, above all, how they are to be explained. Why? is the central question in the analysis of results, just as it is in the analysis of any part of the policy process.

While the analyst needs to look for evidence of the intended results or consequences of a policy or program actually occurring, he or she also needs to look for unintended consequences. In some ways, it is useful if the consequences of nonactions or "paths not taken" can also be discerned. All of this is complicated and tricky. The whole question of how to evaluate policy and program impact will occupy us again in chapter 6.

Relationships Between Major Factors. As figure 2.1 suggests, all major clusters of policy related variables interact with each other. When the major variable clusters are elaborated, as in the discussion accompanying table 2.1, the relationships of any one cluster to all others should be investigated. The world of policy, in fact, seems to be structured that way. In a more practical vein, however, social and political research cannot pay attention to all important factors and relationships in any single study. Therefore, a subset of factors and relationships will be selected for closer analysis in any given study. A few examples of studies using subsets of the basic collection of factors and relationships will indicate the strengths and weaknesses of the particular choices that are made.

The point to be underscored through these illustrations is that any given set of choices about what to study and what not to study in considering policy and policy-relevant variables has both costs and benefits. Practicalities of time, money, and brainpower limit any study. Different choices of what to study and what to exclude are appropriate depending on what needs to be examined with the most care.

Figure 2.2

A Perceptual-Process Model for Investigating Policy Making

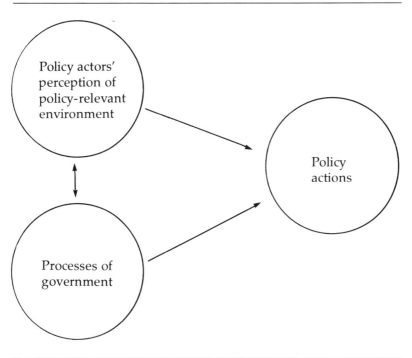

Example A: A Perceptual-Process Model. A model stressing the impact of the perceptions of the policy-relevant environment on the part of policy actors and characteristics of governmental processes on policy actions has been used to investigate the development of four specific federal programs in the economic and human resource development area in the mid-1960s to early 1970s period (Ripley, 1972). The general model used to structure the research is diagrammed in figure 2.2. The point of this example is not to summarize the research findings but to assess the strengths and weaknesses of focusing on these particular variables in trying to explain policy actions.

The model was used, essentially, in analyzing data that can best be described as four case studies of the programs of the Economic Development Administration, of the Job Corps, for Appalachia, and for Model Cities that were systematically compared. The empirical content of the four cases was partly based on judgments—those of the author and those of people involved in decision making for the programs. This model seems best adapted to studies that might be characterized as decision-making studies. The strengths of the model (or more accurately, the strengths of relying on the factors assumed to be most important for purposes of the model) can be summarized briefly:

1. This model allows examination, understanding, and explanation (in a loose sense) of agenda building. In the study cited, the model was applied to the four programs noted above, all of which were created between 1964 and 1966. Thus, the initial stage of the process—agenda building—could be examined in a comparative framework. This is useful since there is relatively little systematic study of agenda building even though it is important (see chapter 4 for more discussion of this point; see also Kingdon, 1984).

2. This model allows examination, understanding, and explanation of initial policy actions (also policy statements). The earliest stages of creating a policy and implementing it

are amenable to use of these particular clusters of important factors.

3. This model accommodates detailed variations in policy actions. These variations might be washed out in a different kind of model and/or a model relying on different kinds of data. Detailed variations might seem trivial, but if policies do not differ a great deal from each other over time (which is often, although not always, the case in the United States), then relatively small variations are or can be important.

4. This model is particularly strong in assessing decision making—not just the content of decisions themselves. A number of approaches to policy studies assume that the content of decisions is all that matters. This model suggests that the manner of decision making also helps produce different kinds of policy actions.

This way of examining policy has some definite limitations:

1. It does not seem particularly suited to dealing with policy results.

2. It may be limited to comparative case studies. And, of course, case studies detailed enough to be worth analysis can be produced only in limited quantities. Therefore, the data base (or the N) is, by design and of necessity, fairly limited.

3. This model—particularly the reliance on perceptions of policy-relevant environment on the part of policy actors—has limited longitudinal utility. Typically, perceptual data have to come from interviews or a combination of interviews and documentary sources. Yet, trying to get interviewees to reconstruct their perceptions for times past is generally unrewarding. They have forgotten the past, or they look at the past through the eyes with which they see the world in the present (which produces distortions, although not necessarily deliberate), or they deliberately distort what they claim to have thought in the past for one or more of many possible reasons.

4. Data collection is costly because considerable detail has to be gathered and because interviewing in general,

which is a technique required for collecting some of the appropriate data, is expensive in terms of both time and financial support.

5. As already implied in some of the points above, the scope of this kind of policy study is limited. As scope expands, detail (and in that sense, rigor) is almost surely going to have to be sacrificed.

This type of model is a good example of the mix of strengths and weaknesses that any particular choice of model is likely to impose on the study of policy. The person or persons doing the study should be aware of those strengths and weaknesses and choose the model best suited to the purpose.

Example B: A Structural Model. One more example will help underscore the general points made above. A submodel focusing on the impact of patterned parts of both the external and internal environment on policy actions and, at least in principle, on policy results in society has here been labeled a structural model (see Ripley and Franklin, 1975, for an example of its use, primarily in explaining dollars available to individual federal agencies that compete in a budget process over time). The general model employed for such a study is portrayed in figure 2.3. Perceptions and processes are omitted. They are replaced by patterned parts of the external environment, by patterned structures inside the government, and by previous policy actions. This model, like the previous example, seeks to explain policy actions. But it goes about seeking those explanations in a very different way. Again, some fairly clear strengths and weaknesses are attached to this way of investigating policy. In some ways, they present a mirror image of the strengths and weaknesses outlined for the first submodel.

The strengths can be summarized in three points:

1. This model is more suitable for investigating ongoing programs than the other model, which is more suitable for investigating new programs in their early stages. The model rests on assumptions and can be made to incorporate research techniques appropriate to continuing programs,

Figure 2.3

A Structural Model for Investigating Policy Making

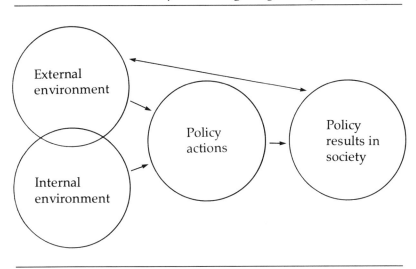

some of them with long histories. Policy actions in such programs and results stemming from them can, in principle, be investigated using this model.

2. This model can be used in connection with data collection priorities that allow both considerable rigor and a large scope (that is, many programs) simultaneously.

3. The first two points imply that this approach to the study of policy allows a long period of time to be covered. People's (policy actors') memories are not a source of data, so relevant policy data can, in principle, be reconstructed for the past from documentary sources. There are, of course, the usual problems in finding comparable data in documentary sources, but the problems do not lie in the decay of people's memories, the distortion of their memories, or the unavailability of the people.

This submodel also has definite limitations:

1. It is not suited to addressing agenda building. It is best at handling ongoing, established programs.

2. It does not examine fine variations in programs; rather, it looks at aggregate program data, which inevitably produces a concern for fairly gross variations.

3. It has no way of probing for, including, or accounting for the various factors (political, psychological, perceptual) that go into the making of any specific decision. It simply assumes these will somehow "wash out" when the aggregate level is investigated.

I do not offer these two examples of models to suggest that one is better than the other in every case, nor am I under any illusion that two examples exhaust the universe of possibilities. But I want to make the point as clearly as I can that analysts have to make choices about what they can study and how they will go about their work. These choices are at many levels and at many points in time. But the first critical choice is to specify a model. Any choice inevitably includes some concerns and excludes others. A choice of a model (or submodel, if you prefer) can shape the nature of the data to be collected and, ultimately, may affect the analytical techniques to be used. The choices of model, data, and analytic techniques influence each other. A good analyst will understand the intricacies and interactions of these choices. A sloppy one will make choices and thereby be forced into additional choices without necessarily knowing or understanding that fact.

Stages of the Policy Process

Numerous treatments of the policy process lay out stages of that process, with various nominal labels attached, in order to help organize discussion and analysis. Such stage-oriented discussions do not form the direct basis for hypothesizing causal relationships, although such hypotheses may emerge. Rather, they are rough chronological and logical guides for observers who want to see impor-

Figure 2.4

The Flow of Policy Stages, Functional Activities, and Products

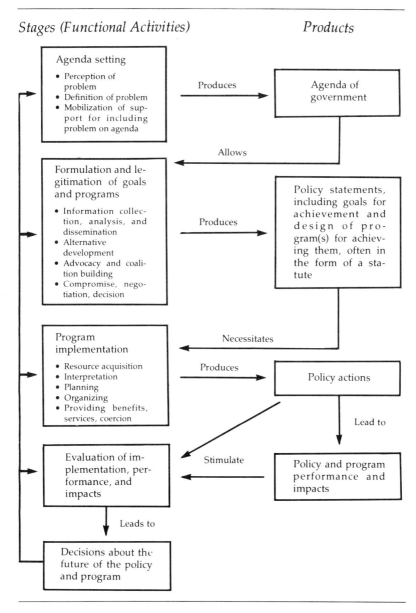

Stages (Functional Activities)   *Products*

Agenda setting

- Perception of problem
- Definition of problem
- Mobilization of support for including problem on agenda

Produces → **Agenda of government**

Allows

Formulation and legitimation of goals and programs

- Information collection, analysis, and dissemination
- Alternative development
- Advocacy and coalition building
- Compromise, negotiation, decision

Produces → **Policy statements, including goals for achievement and design of program(s) for achieving them, often in the form of a statute**

Necessitates

Program implementation

- Resource acquisition
- Interpretation
- Planning
- Organizing
- Providing benefits, services, coercion

Produces → **Policy actions**

Lead to

Evaluation of implementation, performance, and impacts

Stimulate ← **Policy and program performance and impacts**

Leads to

Decisions about the future of the policy and program

49

tant activities in some ordered pattern or sequence. Such organizational helpers are useful and, in fact, essential for anyone trying to plow through the complexities of policy making and policy analysis. At best, such maps—even with their rough spots and simplifications—lend some clarity to the observer/reader/student as he or she grapples with a complicated and sometimes murky set of interactions and processes.

I see no point to repeating a lot of different authors' versions of policy stages. There are many versions. Most of them have some similarities. Many analysts agree pretty well on the central activities requiring attention. Instead, in the final pages of this chapter, I will offer my guide to the stages of the policy process for the readers of this volume.

Major Stages

Figure 2.4 lays out the basic flow of policy stages, major functional activities that occur in those stages, and the products that can be expected at each stage if a product is forthcoming. Naturally, a policy process may be aborted at any stage. Beginning a process does not guarantee that products will emerge or that a stage will be "completed" and so lead to the next stage. Figure 2.4 presents the general flow of stages, activities, and products that can be expected in a policy that is generated and transformed into a viable and ongoing program. "Stages" are the names attached to major clusters of activities that result in identifiable products if they reach conclusion. "Functional activities" are the major subroutines of actions and interactions engaged in by policy actors. "Products" are the output, or end result, of any general stage.

Agenda setting. Somehow the organs of government must decide what they will pay attention to. The stage at which this decision is made in any given policy area is here called agenda setting. Thousands of issues are constantly vying for inclusion on the governmental agenda. Only some of them make it at any given time. The form in which they come on the agenda can vary over time and influence subsequent concrete decisions. The functional activities in the agenda-setting stage include the necessity for some individuals and/or groups to perceive a problem to exist, to decide the government should be involved in the problem, to define the problem, and to mobilize support for including the problem on the governmental agenda.

Competition enters these activities in several ways. First, different people compete to attract the attention of governmental actors for inclusion of any specific problem on the agenda. There is not a fixed number of agenda item "slots" available at any one time. On the other hand, the capacity for the government to include items on its action agenda at any point in time is not unlimited. Second, even within the groups and among individuals concerned with a general issue area there will be competition over the specific definition of the problem and, subsequently, competition over which groups and views to mobilize and how to do it.

Formulation and Legitimation of Goals and Programs. Not all agenda items receive specific treatment in the form of decisions about policies and programs. Not all of them even get translated into a form that allows specific formulation and legitimation activities to take place. But if an item on the agenda is treated in any concrete way, the next step is for it to become the subject of formulation and legitimation.

Formulation and legitimation are complex activities that involve four major sets of functional activities, each complex in its own right. Part of formulating alternatives and then choosing one alternative for possible ratification is collecting, analyzing, and disseminating information for purposes of assessing alternatives and projecting likely outcomes and for purposes of persuasion.

Alternative development is one of the successor subroutines to the one dealing with information. Another is advocacy, in which different persons and groups advocate different points of views and alternatives and seek to build supporting coalitions in support of their views and their preferred alternative. Finally, usually as a result of compromise and negotiation, a decision is reached. If the compromise and negotiation process breaks down, no decision is reached.

The generic products of the formulation and legitimation stage are policy statements (declarations of intent, including some form of goal statement) and the design of programs for making the intent concrete and pursuing achievement of the goals. Both the goals and the program designs may be vague and sketchy. Grandiose goal statements that lack clarity are usually the result of the compromise process. Too much specificity and clarity might prevent compromise of forces that don't really agree on fundamental concrete goals and aspirations. If the goals are raised to a more general and murky level, they can attract the support of persons and groups that might otherwise disagree.

Reasons for lack of specificity and clarity in program design are more numerous. Partly it is a matter of not proliferating details that might also proliferate disagreements, and partly it is a matter of time on the part of Congress, since program designs usually appear first in a statute. Congress must address hundreds, even thousands, of agenda items in any given two-year period. The members cannot fool with any one too long. Throughout the course of history, Congress has gotten into the habit of delegating administrative power to the president and/or to the agencies and secretaries concerned to flesh out rudimentary program designs. From the early 1930s to 1983, Congress could hedge its bets by inserting some form of legislative veto in a statute, which in effect made the president or agency check with Congress before proceeding with some specific actions. The Supreme Court ruled this invention unconstitutional in mid-1983. This ruling may force

Congress to fill in a few more details some of the time, but it is doubtful if it will have more effect than that. The pressures producing extensive delegation by Congress will not change.

Program Implementation. The next stage (assuming that a policy has been stated and a. program created) is program implementation. In order to implement a program, resources need to be acquired. The law needs to be interpreted, usually in written regulations and then in elaborations of those regulations. A variety of planning activities typically take place. Various organizing routines are part of implementation. Finally, the payoff—routines of providing benefits, services, and/or coercion (whatever the tangible manifestation of the program) are developed. All of these activities, although they sound more dull than advocacy and negotiation, are political. Conflict and disagreement can erupt. Various techniques of conflict resolution are necessarily brought into play. Policy actions are the products of the various routines and activities that comprise the program implementation stage.

Evaluation of Implementation, Performance, and Impacts. After policy actions lead to various kinds of results (what I call performance and impact), evaluation of both the actions (implementation) and the results (performance and impacts) takes place. The word *evaluation* often conjures up an image of "objective" social scientists applying rigorous analytic techniques and letting the chips fall where they may. Some of that may transpire. But, as used in this book, evaluation is a much broader concept and refers to the assessment of what has happened or, in many cases, what is *thought* to have happened. The "what" can refer to implementation, to short-run results (performance), or to long-run results (impacts). That assessment takes place constantly and is done by all kinds of people—officials of all descriptions, interest groups, legislators, researchers inside the government, and researchers outside the government. Some evaluation is completely based on political instincts and judgments. A good deal is based on a mix of a little information (often anecdotal) and political judgments. Some (a small portion) is based on systematic analysis of fairly extensive information (data).

Policy analysts coming from political science or any other discipline have a role to play in evaluation of implementation, performance, and impacts. But they should realize that their form of evaluation is only one form and that probably it is less politically relevant than almost any other form of evaluation that takes place. Not too much should be expected in terms of attention to or subsequent actions based on evaluation. On the other hand, evaluation should not be written off entirely. It has a place. I will return to this theme later in the book.

Decisions about the Future of the Policy and Program. The evaluative processes and conclusions, in all of their diversity, lead to one or more of many decisions about the future (or nonfuture) of the policy and program being evaluated. The necessity for such decisions means that the cycle can be entered again at any of its major stages. Conceivably, a problem will be taken off the agenda either because it has been "solved" or because it is viewed as no longer relevant. Or the nature of its most salient features as an agenda item may be changed. Thus, decisions about the future might reset the cycle to the agenda setting stage.

Those decisions may lead back to policy formulation and legitimation. The necessity or legitimacy of keeping an item on the agenda may not be questioned, but legislative (statutory) revisions may be viewed as necessary or desirable, at least by some actors. Thus, the cycle is reentered somewhere in the activity cluster comprising formulation and legitimation. In some cases, decisions about the future may not require new legislation or amendments to existing legislation, but they may require some adjustments in program implementation.

Principal Limits on and Utility of a Stage Conception of the Policy Process

Remember when looking at the policy process as a succession of stages that any such conception is artificial. It may also not be true to what happens. It has a logical appeal, and it is presented chronologically, but chronological reality as it emerges in any case may vary significantly from what the stage-based model says "should" happen in a specific order. The process can be stopped at any point, and, in most cases, the policy process is truncated at some fairly early stage. Only some fairly modest subsets of all possible policies go through the entire process. And the process can be reentered or reactivated at any point and at any time.

In short, reality is messy. Models, particularly a nice listing of stages with an implied tidy chronology, are not messy. In a collision between tidiness and untidiness the analyst must not be so struck by the values of order as to force reality into a model in which it might not fit.

These are only caveats, however. The utility of organizing data and thoughts about complicated reality in this way is great. It allows the analyst to look for patterns and, more important, to explain the causes of different patterns.

Each of the major clusters of policy products contained in figure 2.4 imply the beginning questions that are likely to be central to political scientists who are functioning as policy analysts:

1. The agenda generates the questions: To what does the government pay attention? Why?
2. Policy statements generate the questions: What does the government say it will do? Why?
3. Policy actions generate the questions: What does the government do? Why? How well does it do it?
4. Policy and program performance and impact generate the questions: What differences do government actions make? Why? How well do the programs work? Why?

These are not elaborately worded questions, but they contain the essence of the policy analytic enterprise. Clear answers are hard to come by, especially when they go beyond a fairly simple descriptive level.

Summary

1. Models in general are a useful device for portraying complex reality, including the policy process, in understandable form.

2. The simplest and most general model of the policy process introduces the interrelated concepts of environment, policy actors' perceptions of environment, governmental policy activity, and societal policy activity as the most important.

3. A more complicated model of the policy process necessarily distinguishes between different aspects of the environment, two types of governmental policy activity (policy statements and policy actions), and two types of societal policy activity (societal implementation and policy and program results).

4. The major policy stages are: (1) agenda setting; (2) formulation and legitimation of goals and programs; (3) program implementation; and (4) evaluation of implementation, performance, and impacts.

3
Types of Policy Responses

We have seen in chapter 2 that there are broad commonalities in the policy process that allow an analyst to conceive of relationships in a general sense, regardless of the substantive policies involved. However, the contents of policies obviously vary a great deal. What is not obvious is what differences in policies are systematic enough and important enough to be consistently helpful in explaining different configurations of policy-related phenomena.

Many students of politics and policy have attempted to categorize policy and have come up with a number of categorical schemes that serve, in one way or another, a variety of purposes. In this chapter I will present one scheme of organizing policy types in the United States, which was developed at length in separate studies of formulation and legitimation (Ripley and Franklin, 1984) and implementation (Ripley and Franklin, 1982). It is based on considerable work of other scholars in the last several decades (especially Lowi, 1964 and 1967, and Huntington, 1961; see also Froman, 1968; Hayes, 1981; Lowi, 1972; and Salisbury, 1968).

This scheme meets (or is based on) the following criteria:

1. It covers most instances of domestic, foreign, and defense policy and all of the major recurring types. (It does not, however, pretend to cover all instances of policy.)
2. It has predictive power. Certain relationships occur in predictable fashion in various policy areas.
3. It associates perceptions of policy actors of what is at stake with different kinds of relationships among actors. On this point Lowi posits a one-way causal relationship; for him, the perceptions of what is at stake cause certain predictable configurations of policy actor relationships to emerge. I am more content with an associational statement: predictably different configurations of relationships between policy actors exist in different policy areas characterized by different perceptions of what is at stake. The relationships and the perceptions tend to persist, are interrelated, and tend to support each other.
4. It applies both to formulation and legitimation politics and to the politics of implementation, at least for domestic policy. (And the scheme is generated from the basis of differing perceptions by the policy actors of different kinds of impact.)

This chapter first lays out the seven categories of policy types that are proposed as useful for the policy analyst who is a political scientist. Second, it suggests some predictable patterns of policy-making relationships in policy formulation and legitimation, and third, it suggests the predictable patterns of relationships in implementation.

A Policy Typology

The policy typology I present here as conceptually useful and as having considerable empirical utility for a policy analyst who is also a political scientist stems from the basic perceived intention behind sets of policies. What is the government attempting to do with policy A or policy B? More important, in the debate about the policies or in the perceptions of those who are policy actors (that is, interested in the outcome of the debate), what do the intentions of the policy appear to be? To put the same question another way, what do those involved think is at stake in any given policy discussion or debate?

The scheme for classifying policies depends on the answers to the above questions. The utility of the scheme depends on there being answers that repeat themselves frequently enough so that policies fall into a relatively small number of categories. The scheme relies on the commonality of perceptions at a level of abstraction that allows the analyst to group policies based on those perceptions rather than on the more commonplace notion that some policies affect agriculture, some affect education, some affect foreign aid, some affect housing (and so on to a large number of discrete policy areas).

The scheme presented here has seven different categories of policy: four in the domestic area and three covering options in foreign and defense policy. As with any scheme using only a few categories and covering a rich array of possibilities and human behavior, there may be a few instances that are unclear, a few that simply don't fit, a few that are genuine hybrids, and some instances that change character—and therefore change categories—over time. There is no guarantee that every example of a policy that can be brought forward will fit tidily and unambiguously and unchangingly in one category or another. But most will. And where policies fit several places at once, it is because they try to achieve several different things and are perceived to have put several different kinds of things at stake simultaneously. The perceptions of the actors will be that such policies raise several different general kinds of issues simultaneously. Similarly, where policies appear to the analyst to be moving among categories over time, it is because the perceptions of the actors change over time. What they believe is at stake changes.

The four domestic policy types are called (1) distributive, (2) competitive regulatory, (3) protective regulatory, and (4) redistributive. The three types encompassing foreign and defense policy are (1) structural, (2) strategic, and (3) crisis. Each of the seven types will be defined separately, and illustrations for each will be given.

Domestic Policy Types

Distributive Policy. Distributive policies and programs are intended to promote private activities that are alleged by supporters to be desirable and to be activities that require government support and intervention in the form of a subsidy of some kind, because they would not be undertaken without that subsidy. Subsidies are payments of some kind (not necessarily or exclusively cash in all cases) to induce private actors to engage in desired behavior.

Tangible government benefits constituting the subsidies can include cash. They can also include payments in kind (a major Department of Agriculture program in 1983 and 1984, for example, is called PIK—payment in kind), grants, low-interest loans, provisions in the tax code that require desired behavior in order to provide benefits in the form of forgiven taxation or lower taxation, and licenses or franchises granted to the individuals, groups, or companies that engage in the desired activity (with the license or franchise, in effect, guaranteeing a profit for those individuals, groups, or companies).

Typically, the condition of the subsidy as described in the distributive policy is straightforward; it says to a certain subset of people or group of people that, if they undertake activity A, they will be rewarded with benefit B. Occasionally, the reward will come if a certain activity is not undertaken. A classic example in this vein is an agriculture program that pays farmers in cash or in kind for not producing certain crops. In 1983, this principle was extended for the first time to dairy production. The agricultural products in themselves are good, but overproduction is thought to be undesirable because it depresses prices. Therefore, the subsidy to farmers is based on the condition of limiting certain production. The subsidy, in theory, replaces income that is sacrificed.

Traditionally, until roughly the late 1970s and early 1980s, the perception of distributive policy on the part of policy actors was not of the whole field but rather of each individual policy or program on a disaggregated basis. In other words, there was no sense that any given subsidy affected any other subsidy. The assumption was that all kinds of activities and groups could be subsidized without worrying about the total bill for subsidy. There was no sense among the participants that distributive policy was zero-sum—that is, with a fixed pot against which all subsidies must be charged. If an individual or group lost a struggle to obtain or perpetuate a subsidy, they did not do so because the same resources went to someone else undertaking an activity in a quite different field. Rather, they simply lost because they could not put together a large enough and influential enough coalition to win. Similarly, those who won subsidies were not perceived to do so at the expense of anyone else.

In the late 1970s and 1980s, this image of distributive policy began to change because of the growing realization that resources were not unlimited and that there were at least some aspects of a zero-sum game in distributive policy (and between distributive policies aggregated and other types of policies—all of which cost money). The Budget Act of 1973 set up the machinery that, if used in one way, could force Congress to set a total bottom-line figure for all spending before dividing it up. Prior to that time the bottom line had simply emerged by adding up the individual actions, although presidents had struggled for many years to provide some discipline in the budgetary process through providing a single total figure and suggestions of what individual programs should be funded at what level to reach that total.

The Budget Act itself did not change behavior. Rather, the act provided an institutional framework and process for viewing distributive policy as part of all policy that cost money and, therefore, as not founded on an unlimited resource base. By the late 1970s and particularly by the early 1980s, a number of conditions had changed that forced a zero-sum view on national policy makers, especially Congress, more forcefully. National deficits rose dramatically and were widely agreed to have undesirable consequences. President Jimmy Carter pushed for use of the budget reconciliation process in 1980 and President Ronald Reagan did so even more forcefully in 1981 and 1982. This process, provided for in the Budget Act, underscores the zero-sum nature of decisions, or at least it underscores the costliness of individual decisions even if they are still not treated as strict trade-offs for one another. Simultaneously, the economy sputtered, and recoveries from the sputtering were half-hearted. This also contributed to an increasing awareness that resources are in no way unlimited, even in a country as rich as the United States.

Examples of distributive policies and programs active in the last few decades include the following:

- Cash payments for purchase of agricultural crops to support prices.
- In-kind payments for agricultural crops in exchange for not planting crops.
- Grants to localities for hospital construction, mass transportation facilities, and sewage plants.
- General grants (revenue sharing) to states and localities for a wide variety of purposes at their discretion.
- Financing of water development projects.
- Grants for research purposes to universities.
- Preferred tax treatment for certain kinds of investments.
- Provision of income tax deductions for individuals for interest paid on home mortgages and local property taxes.
- Patents for inventors and copyrights for authors.

- Permits for timbering, mining, and grazing on public lands at rates below those that would be determined in an open market.
- Funding of the interstate highway system.
- Federal guarantees of loans for private corporations in financial trouble (for example, the Chrysler Corporation).

One final word on the Reagan administration. First, although President Reagan made some attacks on some subsidies and did force use of the reconciliation process in budgeting, his administration left many subsidies unchallenged. And even some of those challenged withstood the challenges mostly intact. Second, the Reagan rhetoric identified social programs as subsidies as a way of spurring an attack on them. This may have been effective political rhetoric, but the use of the language of subsidy to describe programs that are redistributive in nature is inaccurate analytically, although perhaps useful in the service of some political values. The analyst must learn not to take political rhetoric, regardless of source, at face value.

Competitive Regulatory Policy. Competitive regulatory policies and programs limit the provision of specific goods and services to one or a few designated deliverers usually chosen from a larger number of potential deliverers who may compete for the designation. The policy sets the framework by which the choice is made. This framework includes the apparatus and the criteria by which choices are made. In this particular type of policy most of the "action" is not in policy formulation and legitimation, which are rare events, but in implementation. All policies necessitate a fair amount of delegated authority from Congress to whatever agencies are charged with administration. This is particularly the case in the competitive regulatory arena.

Two major situations lead to major policies in the competitive regulatory arena. First, the good or service in question is scarce—that is, physical limitations seem to make free entry into the market for providers impossible or unworkable. For example, there are only a finite number of television channels or radio frequencies that can be granted because of the technology built into home receiving sets. Second, the public is perceived to have a substantial stake in the manner (including frequency) with which the good or service is offered. For example, it was long thought, and the thought was incorporated into law, that communities needed stable provision of passenger air service and passenger rail service. These policies and decisions also have protective aspects—that is, airlines were required to meet certain standards of safety and service as a condition of being awarded any routes. But the competitive aspect of regulation was strictly limited to the award of routes to different airlines. Before airline deregulation, only a finite number of airlines could serve any two points, and the Civil Aeronautics Board determined both that finite number and which airlines would win those routes. At least for lucrative routes, there were many more competitors than routes available for award. Less lucrative routes carried a subsidy with them to induce airlines to apply.

These regulations involving the provision of specific goods and services are competitive because there is always the potential for more applicants to want to provide the service (because of its inherent profitability or its subsidized profitability) than there are awards available. The potential service providers compete. Government serves as the referee for the competition by setting up the process, picking the umpires, and establishing the rules under which the competition is decided.

In a sense, competitive regulatory policy is a hybrid. It contains elements of subsidy—the winning providers are typically subsidized either by being awarded a piece of a lucrative market (television channels tend to make lots of money) or by direct government payment for providing certain services (before airline deregulation, airlines made money on routes to small, out-of-the-way places because the government supplemented fares to make sure the routes were profitable). It also contains elements of protective regulation because certain standards must be met in the provision of service (a certain percent of time must be devoted to public service programming by radio or television stations, and there are limits on the percentage of time that can be devoted to commercials).

Historically, federal competitive regulation has been focused on railroads, airlines, barge lines, pipelines, bus lines, truck lines, moving companies, and communications (especially television and radio). In the late 1970s and early 1980s, substantial aspects of most modes of transportation and even some aspects of communications were deregulated. In the case of airlines, they were given the decision-making power over where they would and would not fly, how frequently, and for what price. At the same time some regulations were still necessary. For example, airports can handle only so many flights before their physical facilities are unable to deal with more. Thus airlines had to agree on how to divide up the "slots" at airports where demand for takeoffs and landings exceeded the capacity of the facility. Some protective aspects of the regulation are still in place as of this writing, although the future of these provisions (or who would enforce them) is far from clear.

At this point in the development of public policy on the federal level in the United States, competitive regulation is the least frequently observed type of domestic policy. But, it is here argued that it generates some distinctive political patterns worth the attention of a political scientist who is a policy analyst.

A number of examples of competitive regulatory policy have been mentioned above. And, because of the spread of deregulation in this policy area, some of the major examples of past decades are limited to those decades and do not apply, at least at the moment. These examples include:

- Authorization of specific railroads, bus lines, and airlines to operate specific routes (coupled with a requirement that they *must* operate them).

- Authorization of specific trucking lines to operate specific routes for specific commodities.
- Authorization for the operation of specific television channels and radio frequencies by specified operators/owners.

Protective Regulatory Policy. Protective regulatory policies and programs are designed to protect the public by setting the conditions under which various private activities can and cannot take place. Conditions that are thought to be harmful to the general public or major portions of it are prohibited. Such conditions include pollution of air and water, release of unsafe drugs onto the market, sale of adulterated and unhealthy food, overly long working hours, and unsafe work places. Conditions that are thought to be necessary to protect the general public or major portions of it are required. For example, banks, department stores, and other institutions giving credit must disclose the true interest rate they charge. Airplanes must be certified as safe before they can be flown in commercial service.

Rate setting is also part of protective regulation. In cases in which the government is involved in rate setting (as it used to be for airlines, railroads, truck lines, and all producers of natural gas), the services or goods can be provided only at the specified rates. The "protection" offered the public is not as apparent as that prohibiting the sale of unsanitary food that may cause disease or requiring that people be informed about what interest they are being charged for borrowing money. Rather, the "protection" is the provision of "fair" rates for a particular good or service. The standards of "fairness" are, typically, elaborate and are the subject of continuing political debate and struggle, both during formulation and legitimation and during implementation.

The urge to "deregulate" has occasioned considerable political debate over the years of the late 1970s and particularly into the 1980s. However, unlike the debate over deregulation in competitive regulatory matters, agreement to lessen protective regulation has been far more difficult to achieve and has been the occasion for considerable disagreement and sharp political controversy. In competitive regulatory matters, agreement on the desirability of deregulation was reasonably widespread, and deregulation was relatively easy to achieve. In protective regulatory areas, feelings run high on both sides and movement is difficult and politically charged. Only in areas of rate setting when it is attached to competitive deregulation—as with airlines, railroads, and trucks—has elimination of protective regulation been relatively easy to achieve. And rate setting in itself is still controversial, as the case of natural gas vividly illustrates.

Examples of protective regulatory policies and programs include:

- Licensing of drugs before they can be sold.
- Inspection of food processing.
- Penalties on owners and manufacturers of cars that emit more than a certain level of pollutants.
- Penalties on manufacturers of cars that do not meet certain mileage standards for fuel efficiency.
- High taxes to reduce the use of certain scarce resources such as oil.
- High taxes to reduce the use of certain harmful goods such as alcohol or tobacco.
- Setting of rates for airlines, railroads, bus lines, trucking companies, barge lines, and pipelines.
- Bans on harmful food additives such as Red Dye No. 2 and saccharin.
- Bans on unfair business or labor practices.
- Prohibition of business agreements that restrain competition.
- Requirements that grantors of credit disclose true interest rates.
- Requirements that certain information about governmental decisions be publicly available.

- Requirements that certain information about individuals in private files (such as those of credit companies or insurance companies) be available to the individuals concerned.
- Requirements of minimum wages and maximum hours for workers.
- Specification of postmining restoration that must be accomplished by strip-mining companies.
- Controls over wages and prices.

Redistributive Policy. Redistributive policies and programs are perceived to result in the shifting of wealth, property, rights, or other values among social classes or racial groups in society. There are perceived winners and losers. That is, redistribution is perceived to take place to the benefit of one or more classes and racial groups and, simultaneously, at the expense of some other class or classes and/or racial group or groups. For example, some whites and their spokespersons may perceive moves to strengthen rights for racial and ethnic minorities as redistributive at their expense. Wealthy people may perceive certain kinds of taxes (progressive taxes on personal income, taxes on capital gains) coupled with the use of tax revenues for programs for the poor, such as food stamps or welfare, as redistributive at their expense. Some males may perceive affirmative action programs aimed at increasing female employment, particularly in nontraditional or in higher level positions, as redistributive at their expense.

One of the fascinating features of American politics is that, although redistribution can, and in fact does, run in the direction of giving additional privileges to the already privileged at the expense of already deprived, political debate rarely treats such instances as redistributive. There are debates over such policies, but not in the same terms. Those in favor of such policies (President Reagan, for example) excoriate the less well-off for being beneficiaries of subsidies and being part of "iron triangles" that guarantee them benefits that produce unbalanced and irresponsible federal budgets. Some of the opponents of such policies talk in terms of "fairness," which is getting close to the language of redistribution. But there are no sustained debates over such policies in terms of redistribution. The closest we have come to such a debate in recent years was over President Reagan's tax proposals in 1981. Even then the debate sputtered and was not productive of redistributive politics. In fact, many seemed to buy President Reagan's assertion that a tax system should not be used for redistributive purposes. What Reagan meant was that the progressive features of the federal income tax should be diminished, but he showed no awareness of the fact that any tax system has some sort of redistributive impact in some direction. And his opponents did not force him to admit that truth because they did not conceive of the debate in those terms either.

Redistributive debate, then, in the United States tends to be over policies perceived, in simple language, to take from the rich and give to the poor (this rough characterization can also cover matters of racial, gender, or ethnic equality). One would assume that, in a reasonably open democracy, those with less, economically speaking, would by virtue of greater numbers tend to dominate politics and propel policy in a generally redistributive direction. Such has not been the case in the United States. Some redistributive policies have been enacted from time to time, and some programs have been created to implement those policies. But some have also been abandoned, and others have been cut back. Some have been defeated for a long period of time before being tried. Some have been defeated consistently and never been tried at all. And policies that work in favor of the already advantaged individuals and groups continue to be adopted. In short, the total mix of U.S. domestic policy is only mildly redistributive toward the less advantaged in a few areas and is fairly strongly redistributive in favor of the already advantaged in a number of other areas (Page, 1983).

The reasons for this relatively lopsided, or asymmetrical, perception of what is and what is not redistributive stems from a variety of causes. Chief among them are the lack of a genuine working-class party in the United States, the relative lack of economic class distinctions in people's perceptions and even in their self-identifications, and continuing belief in progress, self-reliance, "free enterprise," and severely limited government. The reasons are interesting, but need not detain us here. We need only to note that the analyst should expect a different kind of debate over redistribution in the United States from the debate that occurs in most Western European societies.

Examples of redistributive policy, defined in this uniquely American way, include:

- Progressive personal income tax rates coupled with spending programs that do not return the benefits to the most heavily taxed.
- Prohibition of racial or gender discrimination in employment (perhaps coupled with affirmative action requirements).
- Government-sponsored health care for the indigent.
- Income maintenance for the poorest people in society through such devices as welfare, tax credits, and a negative income tax.
- Employment and training programs limited to the poor.
- Food stamps for the disadvantaged.

One other pervasive dynamic feature of American politics needs to be noted in connection with redistributive policy. Whenever a policy that genuinely redistributes to the poorer or more deprived groups is established, there is considerable pressure, seemingly immediate and automatic, to extend the benefits to everyone, not just to the most deprived. Sometimes such an extension is accorded in creating the policy and program as the political price that must be paid in order to obtain initial passage. Sometimes such broadening of eligible beneficiaries occurs after the program is established, usually as a way of bowing to great political pressure and as a political guarantee of program survival. Thus, programs conceived of as redistributive in the first instance may well become distributive. Examples abound—the Model Cities program, the Economic Development program, the Appalachian program, Medicare, and some aspects of programs generated by the Comprehensive Employment and Training Act (CETA) and its successor, the Job Training Partnership Act (JTPA).

Model Cities began life targeted on the most deprived neighborhoods in a few cities. It expanded within individual cities so that less deprived neighborhoods could also benefit, and the number of designated cities was also expanded. The definition of economically deprived areas eligible for the Economic Development program expanded so that more than four-fifths of the entire country became eligible. The Appalachian program expanded both in its definition of Appalachia—some parts of the country included in the designation were well out of view of the mountains that gave the region its name—and by virtue of being imitated by a variety of other regional commissions taking in many other parts of the country. Medicare made everyone eligible from the start, not just those who were medically indigent, and there was no sliding scale of payments based on ability to pay. Both CETA and JTPA were targeted for the most part to disadvantaged people. But, under CETA, as the public service component of the program expanded in response to economic recession, a number of generally nondisadvantaged people became beneficiaries. JTPA began life with a provision that 10 percent of the money could be used for so-called displaced workers, virtually all of whom were not disadvantaged using the traditional criteria that had developed in the employment and training field in the 1960s and 1970s.

Foreign and Defense Policy Types

Structural Policy. Structural policies are aimed primarily at procuring, deploying, and organizing military personnel and materiel. A few, such as use of surplus food for export for political purposes, are out of the military areas. Presumably, these activities take place within the framework of decisions about strategy already made.

By definition, these policies and programs are distributive, since the federal government totally subsidizes defense. But the details of who gets subsidized, how much is spent, and when it is spent all need to be decided. Sometimes these policies are debated as if the actors, at least those critical of certain decisions or programs, realize that subsidy represents a great deal of what is at stake here. Proponents of certain programs (subsidies), of course, make the most of the contribution of those programs to strengthening the national defense.

Examples of this kind of foreign and defense policy include:

- Procurement decisions involving specific weapons systems and specific suppliers. There is also an element of competition here in that for any specific decision there are likely to be several suppliers who want the contract.
- The creation or closing of military installations, especially in the United States. Considerations both of location and of size are particularly important in these decisions.
- Decisions on size and location and composition of reserve forces.
- Decisions about what agricultural surpluses to send to what countries.

Perhaps the single clearest defining characteristic of structural programs is that they intimately and obviously involve important economic interests in the United States, whether those be in the defense industry, localities dependent on military bases for a good part of the local payroll, or American farmers who make money if wheat goes to the Soviet Union and lose money if it doesn't.

Strategic Policy. Strategic policies and programs are perceived to assert and to provide for the implementation of the basic military and foreign policy stance of the United States toward other nations, in clusters and individually. "Foreign policy" in its classic sense and "defense posture" in its classic sense both encompass strategic policy. Examples include:

- Decisions about the basic mix of military forces on the part of the United States; the relationship of different weapons systems to each other; the relationship of bomber-based, land-based, and submarine-based nuclear missiles; and the existence, number, and location of MX missiles.
- Decisions about the U.S. position on disarmament in international negotiations.
- Decisions about the U.S. position on human rights in international negotiations.
- Decisions about the size and location of U.S. overseas forces (for example, troop strength in Western Europe and Korea) and decisions about the deployment of cruise and Pershing missiles in Western Europe.
- Immigration: the status of political refugees and the status of "undocumented" workers from Mexico, Latin America, other locations.
- Foreign aid: recipients, amounts, and type (economic, military).
- Foreign trade: quotas, tariffs, requests for export limits from other countries, and U.S. export policy.
- Sales of arms to foreign nations.
- U.S. presence in and stance toward unstable foreign situations; for example, Central America and the Middle East.

Crisis Policy. Crisis policies are responses to immediate problems for the United States that are of foreign origin.

These problems are perceived to be serious for the United States. They seem to arise with little or no warning (or at least policy actors were oblivious to the warning signals), and they demand immediate response. Trouble areas may well be known before a crisis erupts, but the exact timing and nature of the cause of a crisis cannot be predicted. For example, it was obvious to many, including the United States government at the highest levels, that relations between the United States and Japan in 1941 were not good. However, the Japanese attack on Pearl Harbor was a surprise and generated a crisis. Similarly, that the Middle East had been unstable for many decades was not a secret to policy makers in the United States or in any other country that cared about the region. The timing and nature of the Israeli invasion of southern Lebanon in mid-1982 was not predictable and created a crisis for the United States (although the response demanded was less immediate and apparent than that demanded in the case of the Japanese attack on Hawaii). Examples of crises include:

- The Japanese attack on Pearl Harbor in 1941.
- The impending French collapse in Indochina in 1954.
- The British and French attack on Suez in 1956.
- The Soviet Union's placement of missiles in Cuba in 1962.
- North Korea's seizure of a U.S. Navy ship in 1968.
- Cambodia's seizure of a U.S. merchant ship in 1975.
- Iran's seizure of the U.S. embassy and hostages in 1979.
- Soviet invasion of Afghanistan in 1979.
- Israel's invasion of Lebanon in 1982.

Relationships in Formulation and Legitimation

The foregoing taxonomy of policies (or any other taxonomy) has no particular utility unless it helps observers and analysts understand patterns and, through that understanding, make predictions. The reason I find this particular classification useful is that it is tied to patterns of political relationships, both in formulation and legitimation processes *and* in implementation processes. These patterns are regular and therefore allow some prediction. They are not presented as perfect, completely refined, and final, but they are presented as faithful to a wide range of empirical reality and as worth further conceptual refining and empirical testing.

What can be said of the most important relationships in formulation and legitimation that vary systematically by policy type? The following few pages do not attempt to present all of the variations (for a much fuller treatment, see Ripley and Franklin, 1984), but only those most important for a reader of this book trying to get a basic feel for policy analysis in political science. More details will be added in chapter 4, which focuses on the study of agenda building, formulation, and legitimation. In discussing both formulation and legitimation relationships in this section and implementation relationships in the next section, five points will be discussed: the identity of the principal actors; the nature of the relationships among the actors; the stability of the relationships among the actors; the degree of conflict among the actors; and the general degree and weight of influence over decisions flowing between the actors.

In the discussion of the relationships in formulation and legitimation, six of the seven types of policy are used. Competitive regulatory policy is omitted for two reasons. First, there are only a few occasions on which such policy is formulated in a general, statutory sense. For the most part, competitive regulatory policy is implemented on a case-by-case basis by the agencies given responsibility for such implementation through statutes. Second, with the onset of the popularity of deregulation in the late 1970s and into the 1980s, there is even less immediate likelihood of formulation and legitimation activities leading to competitive regulation. The formulation and legitimation activities that have

Table 3.1

Principal Actors and Relationships in Formulation and Legitimation by Policy Type

Policy Type	Principal Actors	Relationships among the Actors	Stability of Relationships	Degree of Conflict among the Actors During Decision Making
Distributive	Congressional subcommittees; executive bureaus; small interest groups	Mutual support of individual programs; logrolling between programs (everyone gains)	Stable	Low
Protective Regulatory	Congressional subcommittees and committees; full House and Senate; executive agencies; trade associations; consumer groups	Bargaining; compromise	Unstable	Moderate

Policy Type	Principal Actors	Relationships among the Actors	Stability of Relationships	Degree of Conflict among the Actors During Decision Making
Redistributive	President and his appointees; committees and/or Congress; largest interest groups (peak associations)	Ideological and class conflict	Stable	High
Structural	Congressional subcommittees; executive bureaus; small interest groups	Mutual support of individual programs; logrolling between programs (everyone gains)	Stable	Low
Strategic	Executive agencies; president; Congress	Bargaining; compromise	Unstable	Moderate
Crisis	President and advisers	Cooperation	Unstable	Varies. Private disagreements can be low to high. Public disagreements also range from low to high and come after the decision.

occurred in the last few years have all run in the other direction (that is, competitive deregulation).

Table 3.1 summarizes the most salient points about the identity of the principal actors, the nature of the relationships among the actors, the stability of those relationships, and the degree of conflict among the actors. These points are discussed in the following sections.

The Principal Actors

In distributive policy the principal congressional actors are clustered in subcommittees. Specific distributive policies and programs are typically under the purview of one subcommittee in the House and another in the Senate. The major executive branch actors are clustered, typically, in a single bureau with responsibility for the policy or program in question. There is substantial interest group participation in the formulation and legitimation of most distributive policies and programs. The interest groups tend to be relatively small and are built around specific policies and programs. Sometimes larger interest groups that deal with aggregations of specific interests also take positions and are active in distributive program areas.

In protective regulatory policy, congressional subcommittees are important actors as are the full committees with jurisdiction over the policy or program under debate. The full House and Senate also become important actors in this policy arena, since issues typically do not get resolved short of the floor as they often do in the distributive arena. In the executive branch, full executive agencies, including the central leadership, not just the individual bureaus, are the usual actors. In the private sector, trade associations for those to be regulated and, to a lesser extent, consumer groups pressing for regulation are the typical interest group participants.

In the area of redistributive policy formulation and legitimation, the congressional actors tend not to be at the subcommittee level but rather at the level of full committees or, more frequently, at the level of the full House and Senate. In the executive branch, the president often gets personally involved. His appointees, both on his own staff and in the various executive branch agencies, also regularly get involved. The private groups that are involved tend to be the largest interest groups, aggregations of organizations, individuals, and groups of individuals with at least some interests in common—so-called peak associations.

The principal actors who make structural foreign and defense policy are the same as those who make distributive domestic policy. The principal congressional participants are subcommittees. Bureaus in the executive branch are major actors, and relatively small interest groups, representing those who benefit from the federal largesse in structural policy, are the major private sector participants.

In strategic policy, the major forces are the president and the relevant executive agencies (not disaggregated into individual relatively small bureaus). Congress as a whole, on the floor of the House and Senate, also gets involved, almost always reacting to a presidential initiative.

Crisis policy involving foreign and defense matters really involves only the president, his closest advisors on foreign and defense policy, and those few individuals he feels he wants to consult. Those individuals vary by president. What's done in the way of consultation also depends on the amount of time the president feels he has for response to the crisis situation.

Relationships among the Actors

In distributive policy, the principal actors tend to agree with one another that the policy and programs they mutually support are important and deserving. Thus, each policy or program area tends to be supported by a "subgovernment" of like-minded individuals in subcommittees of Congress, bureaus in the executive branch, and interest groups representing those individuals and corporate entities that stand to gain directly from the programs. Between these different subgovernments there often is little contact. But, at minimum, there is an implicit logroll between the different subgovernments. That is, they agree—often without talking about it—to support one another's interests or, at least, not to challenge them. Thus each subgovernment proceeds to get what it can for itself without direct interference from any other interests and sometimes with their direct support.

Protective regulatory policy is usually the subject of controversy. Different actors have different views of what is or is not needed. Typically, those different views are reconciled through a process of bargaining that results in compromise between parties with different views and conflicting interests.

Debate and conflict over redistributive policy tends to be ideological and represents class or racial conflict. Sometimes compromise will produce results, but more often the stronger side wins and the losing side regroups for the day when its ideological and class interests are in a position to dominate. Then the policy can be repealed or at least substantially amended and watered down (or created, depending on which interest won the first time). These issues tend never to be part of a permanent settlement. Instead, they are issues that constantly recur. The sizes of the political coalitions, which usually are two in number, vary, and thus the outcomes vary, depending on the stronger coalition at any point in time.

Again, structural policy parallels distributive policy. The actors working on individual decisions tend to be mutually supportive of the same interests. And there is, at least implicitly, a logroll among the supporters of different discrete policies and programs.

On strategic matters, there are often disagreements. But the actors seek to bargain and usually arrive at compromises. These may take a long time to work out and may change over time—as has been the case with both the B-1 bomber and the MX missile in the last few decades, for example.

In crisis situations there may be private disagreement, but typically the people called by the president to counsel with him will try to be cooperative with him and with each other. Often he will summon people with a history of such cooperation, so there tends to be a self-fulfilling quality to the stress on cooperation. And even if some disagreement takes place in private, there is normally insistence on the part of the president that a united face be presented to Congress and the public. The few members of Congress that are sometimes informed in the early stages of a crisis are picked in part because they are perceived to understand the necessity of cooperation and the limits on disagreement.

Stability of the Relationships

"Stability" is here used to connote the predictability of the substantive positions taken by different coalitions. Do the same coalitions tend to exist in a policy area? Do the coalitions tend to take the same predictable substantive positions? Defined this way, the stable areas, in which the same coalitions and the same substantive positions recur, involve distributive policy, redistributive policy, and structural policy. In the case of distributive and structural policy and programs, the same "subgovernments" tend to persist and to support the same interests. No stability is perfect, of course, and changes do occur, but on a scale running from highly unstable to highly stable these policy areas tend to be toward the stable end. Redistributive policy relationships are stable because the debate is ideological, and the same groups tend to keep the same ideology over time and to coalesce with those who share the basic tenets of that ideology. For example, the debate over publicly funded medical care ("socialized medicine," if you oppose it) has gone on for many decades with the same basic coalitions facing each other year after year and decade after decade. Specific outcomes occur only rarely, although they can change depending on election results.

The other three policy areas—protective regulatory, strategic, and crisis—are all relatively unstable. In the protective regulatory arena there are shifting coalitions, with individuals, committees, groups, and even agencies taking different positions in different debates or taking a position in one debate and sitting out another one. The same general characterization applies to strategic policy. In the crisis arena, the structure for decision making is such that there is no room for coalition formation, and, by definition, different crises pose at least partially unique substantive questions. Thus, there is no element of stability except in cases involving some of the same issues in which the same president happens to be involved. But, of course, the presidency changes hands with some frequency, so even that element of stability is often not present. Like the occasion for decision making itself—the crisis—the response is volatile.

Conflict Between the Actors

The degree of conflict between the actors varies predictably by policy area. In both distributive and structural policy it is predictably low, because subgovernments tend to dominate outcomes. They agree internally, so there is little or no occasion for conflict. And, much of the time, they either do not comment on the claims of other subgovernments or they may overtly support them.

In both protective regulatory and strategic policy there is moderate conflict between the actors during decision making. Often these conflicts are noisy and heated. But the adjective *moderate* seems appropriate because usually the parties closest to the decision making (that is, with the most influence) are willing to bargain toward some sort of compromise outcome. Some of the public rhetoric of those actors may not sound as if it would allow compromise. And the rhetoric of some of those not terribly close to the decision making certainly suggests that compromise would not be possible if they were in charge. But, overall, the conflict is moderate enough to allow compromises and concrete results much of the time.

Conflict over redistributive policy is high. This is because it is based on ideological and class conflicts, and the contending parties are visible coalitions of important and visible policy makers such as the president, leading congressional figures, and the spokespersons for the largest interest groups. Occasionally there are outcomes, but there are also lots of stalemates and standoffs. Even if one side or the other wins in a given struggle, that decision is subject to revision.

In policy making in response to crises, the amount of conflict varies. During the policy making itself, private conflict may be high or low, although it tends to be low. The short-run public conflict among those who make the decision is almost always low. Public conflict after the fact of the decision can vary from high to low, but it is, of course, too late to do anything to affect the decision (although such debates often have some influence on reactions to future crisis situations).

Relationships in Implementation

What relationships vary consistently in implementation processes? I will treat briefly the same areas of generalization that I did in the preceding section with respect to formulation and legitimation. However, here I will treat only the domestic types of policy (and will add a focus on competitive regulatory policy, too, since it is much more present in implementation than in formulation and legitimation). Implementation of much foreign and defense policy is by the military or by the foreign service—many members of both are stationed abroad—and by virtue of the nature of the reaction of foreign governments. Thus, implementation in the foreign and defense sphere, once defense procurement and base closings are excluded, has dif-

Table 3.2

Principal Actors and Relationships in Implementation by Policy Type

Policy Type	Principal Actors	Relationships among the Actors	Stability of the Relationships	Degree of Conflict among the Actors
Distributive	Central federal, federal field, and state and local bureaucracies; producer interests; Congress sporadically	Bureaucrats and beneficiaries arrive at agreeable arrangements	Stable	Low
Competitive Regulatory	Central federal bureaucracy; producer interests; some consumer interests; Congress sporadically	Bureaucrats and potential beneficiaries maintain formal distance; may work closely informally to arrive at mutually satisfactory arrangements	Unstable	Low, with short, higher bursts

Policy Type	Principal Actors	Relationships among the Actors	Stability of the Relationships	Degree of Conflict among the Actors
Protective Regulatory	Central federal and federal field bureaucracies; producer interests; consumer interests; Congress sporadically	Bureaucrats tend to be close to one set of competing interests and distant from or hostile to the other set. Relations based on ideological agreements and disagreements	Unstable	Moderate, with some sustained higher bursts
Redistributive	Federal field and state and local bureaucracies; dependent class and minority groups; ideological groups opposed to benefits; Congress sporadically	Central federal bureaucrats distant from dependent classes/minority groups. State and local bureaucracies have supportive or hostile relations with beneficiaries and groups opposing them. Relations based on ideology	Stable, with unstable elements over time in the bureaucracy	Moderate to high

ferent sets of actors and operates in different political cultures much of the time. Although implementation in those spheres is important and interesting, it is too different to be examined by means of the kinds of conceptual generalizations I make here and the kinds of empirical materials that appear in the literature on implementation most of the time. As analyzed thus far, implementation is really a phenomenon related to domestic policy.

Table 3.2 summarizes the most salient points about the identity of the principal actors, the nature of the relationships among those actors, the stability of the relationships, and the degree of conflict among the actors. These points are discussed more fully in the sections that follow.

The Principal Actors

Bureaucrats at all levels are involved in implementing distributive policy. These can be conceived of as being in three major geographical configurations. A major set of bureaucrats exists in Washington. There is another set in federal field offices (the configuration of which varies from agency to agency). And there are a wide array of bureaucrats at all of the state and local levels in the country. Despite nominally being in the employ of states and localities, many of them in fact are involved in implementing federal programs.

The beneficiaries of distributive policy are the producer interests. They are heavily involved. All producers of a specific type may be involved (or, more likely, represented by some group or groups) if benefits are unlimited or are granted as a matter of right. Only some producers may be involved or represented if benefits are limited or if they are apportioned on a competitive basis, which happens occasionally.

Congress (or, more to the point, subcommittees and individuals in Congress) is involved in implementation matters sporadically, typically when a constituent or group of constituents is involved.

The principal bureaucratic actors in competitive regulatory implementation are located in Washington. Groups representing producer interests and those representing consumer interests (those who receive regulated services) are both important. Congress, again, is sporadically involved, its involvement usually triggered by the appeal of specific constituency-based interests.

In dealing with the implementation of protective regulatory policy, the principal bureaucratic actors are federal bureaucrats both in Washington and in various field offices. Again, producer groups (those regulated) and consumer groups (those presumed to benefit from the regulations) are involved as major actors. Congress gets involved in protective regulatory implementation questions only sporadically. In this policy area such involvement tends to be triggered by complaints from constituents of either excessive or absent zeal on the part of the implementing bureaucrats.

Redistributive program implementation involves all three levels of bureaucracies: Washington, federal field offices, and state and local field offices. Groups representing beneficiaries (best conceived of as dependent classes and minority groups) and ideological groups opposing the legitimacy of benefits in the program are both involved. Congress sporadically oversees and intervenes in implementation matters in this policy area, and there is some examination of impact on beneficiaries, often based on anecdotal evidence.

Relationships among the Actors

In distributive implementation, the federal bureaucracy is typically close to national groups that represent beneficiaries. Federal field bureaucrats and state and local bureaucrats are usually close to local groups representing beneficiaries at that level. This two-way relationship between beneficiaries (who are, if you recall, producers in the case of distributive policy) and bureaucrats is by far the most consistently important in the distributive arena and helps shape many of the implementation decisions.

In the competitive regulatory area, the federal bureaucracy in Washington maintains formal distance from the regulated interests. However, the bureaucrats and regulated interests may work closely together informally to arrive at mutually satisfactory arrangements. This relationship, whatever precise form it may take in any specific instance of competitive regulation, is the most consistently important.

Protective regulatory matters tend to ally federal bureaucrats, both in Washington and in the field, with one set of interests and, therefore, they are at least partially out of sympathy with competing sets of interests. Federal bureaucracies with different interests (one allied with producers, one with consumers, and so on) may change their allegiances over time. The nature of alliances at any given time is related to ideological stances and preferences of the various parties.

Redistributive alliances are also based on ideological agreements and disagreements since class-based and racially based matters are addressed during implementation. All three levels of bureaucracy (they may and probably do vary between them) have either mutually supportive or mutually hostile relationships with groups representing beneficiaries (these beneficiaries are generally minorities and dependent classes). Ideological groups that oppose the beneficiary groups also have some access to bureaucrats as they make implementation decisions.

Stability of the Relationships

"Stability" is used here to indicate the predictability of substantive positions taken and of the identity of individual partners in coalitions. Both distributive policy and redistributive policy implementation are characterized by a high degree of stability. In distributive policy it is predictable that the beneficiaries (producer interests) and the various levels of implementing bureaucracies will tend to agree on procedures, desired outcomes, and so on. Stress between them will be minimal, and in any given program the identity of the principal participants will remain the same.

In redistributive policy the hostility of the groups representing beneficiaries and those groups opposed to them will be predictable and characterized by the presence of the same groups on opposing sides. In the short run the stance of the involved bureaucracies and their relations with the competing sets of groups will appear to be stable. However, over time and largely dependent both on shifting general political moods and particularly on the results of presidential elections that may result in both party and ideological changes, the alliances and allegiances of the different bureaucracies may change. In fact, the results of state and local elections (especially those for governor) may result in more rapid changes in the alliance of state and local bureaucracies than is the case on the federal level.

The elements of instability are even greater in the two regulatory arenas. Election results for president and even for Congress help change the commitments of the federal bureaucracies that are involved. And both types of regulation are characterized by competition, which means that the groups may change their own alliances, and therefore the composition of coalitions is likely to change. This is more evident in competitive regulation, where, by definition for at least the short run, different companies and bidders are pitted against one another in zero-sum games. But even in protective regulation, the positions of all individual components in the private sector are not totally predictable.

Conflict Between the Actors

Conflict is typically low in the cases of implementation of distributive programs. Operating routines to deliver the benefits are viewed as central by all of the principal actors, and they tend to agree that no roadblocks should be placed in front of such delivery. Few issues create conflict.

Conflict is also typically low in the case of competitive regulation. Operating routines designed both to allow the making of competitive decisions and review the performance of awardees are the most important matters. Often there is agreement on what these routines should be. However, short bursts of heated conflict can occur if there is disagreement over such routines and over the standards used either for decisions or for review.

There tends to be consistent and at least moderately intense conflict over the implementation of protective regulatory policy. Federal implementers (bureaucrats) are necessarily enforcers of regulations and limits on the regulated, and that position inevitably breeds a sustained level of conflict. Occasionally, the disagreements will become strong enough that the conflict can rise to a high level for a sustained period of time in some specific program.

Conflict over the implementation of redistributive policy is always moderate and often high. Ideological issues are at stake, and such issues always generate substantial conflict.

Summary

1. Individual policies are not all unique even though they cover a broad substantive range. They can be clustered around the broad intentions of specific policies, which are, in part, defined by the perceptions of policy actors of what is at stake. Only if policies are aggregated into some sort of categories can comparative analysis that goes well beyond case studies take place.

2. The scheme that is presented here develops seven categories of policy. The four domestic policy types are (1) distributive, (2) competitive regulatory, (3) protective regulatory, and (4) redistributive. The three foreign and defense policy types are (1) structural, (2) strategic, and (3) crisis.

3. Each of the policy types generates different, generally predictable patterns involving policy actors. The identity of principal actors, the nature of their relationships with each other, the stability of those relationships, and the degree of conflict among the actors during decision making can be characterized for each of the seven policy types. This is true both during the formulation and legitimation of policy and during the implementation of programs.

4

Agenda Building, Formulation, and Legitimation

The study of formulation and legitimation of policy has long been a bread-and-butter area for political scientists in the United States, although the formal label of "formulation and legitimation" is not universal. Other names might include adoption, incubation, alternative development, and selection. But, as John Locke remarks in *The Second Treatise of Civil Government*, "So the thing be understood, I am indifferent as to the name."

Like Moliere's Monsieur Jourdain, political scientists have been speaking the prose of formulation and legitimation for decades, but they have become more self-conscious of what they are doing in recent years. The whole genre of "A Bill Becomes a Law" books (for the best example, see Bailey, 1950) deals with formulation and legitimation. The best of them also deal with agenda building or agenda setting.

Any attempt to divide the policy process into stages is, by definition, somewhat arbitrary. Reality is rarely as tidy as the mind of an analyst. (If the mind of the analyst is untidier than reality, that analyst is probably in deep trouble!) In some ways the policy process in the United States is a seamless whole. One event leads to another.

Or, more accurately, one event leads to several others, which also influence one another as well as subsequent developments. Confusion and complexity abound. Any attempt at finding seams will have some artificiality to it. The seams will certainly not be straight or unambiguous in their location.

As is laid out in chapter 2, providing a "model" of the policy process and conceiving of the process as a series of logical "stages" both make sense. In that chapter I described five major stages (see figure 2.4 to refresh your memory):

1. agenda setting (I mean the same thing here by agenda building)
2. formulation and legitimation of goals and programs
3. program implementation
4. evaluation of implementation, performance, and impacts
5. decisions about the future of the policy and program

In this chapter, I will further explore some aspects of the first two stages. In chapter 5, I will explore the third stage in more detail, and in chapter 6, I will present the whole topic of evaluation (the fourth stage). The fifth stage is not distinguishable in practice from the earlier stages and leads back into them. It does not require separate discussion.

Some Introductory Considerations

The Notion of the Undertaking

Although I will continue to use the terminology of stages for the purpose of organizing this inquiry in how to conceive of the policy process in the United States, I also want to introduce the notion of the "undertaking" as a way of thinking about policy. The concept itself is useful in trying to grasp the interrelatedness of different pieces of reality, although the pieces still have to be separated for analytical purposes. Those pieces are what I call stages.

The notion of the undertaking with reference to foreign policy was introduced some years ago by Rosenau (1968: 222). He defined it as follows: "An undertaking is conceived to be a course of action that the duly constituted officials of a national society pursue in order to preserve or alter a situation in the international system in such a way that it is consistent with a goal or goals decided upon by them or their predecessors." In a footnote Rosenau says he finds that the concept would also apply to domestic policy.

I like the notion of the "undertaking" because it is broad, flexible, and contains an image of a series of interrelated policy-related events over a possibly substantial period of time. The concept of the "undertaking" can be expanded to incorporate the processes of agenda building, formulation and legitimation, implementation, and evaluation over time. For purposes of thinking about both the domestic and foreign and defense policies of the United States at the national level, a new definition of the undertaking, based on Rosenau's, is needed. I propose the following alteration. A domestic or foreign/defense policy undertaking is a course of action primarily designed by, approved by, and implemented by the duly constituted executive and legislative officials at the national level and by bureaucratic officials at the national, state, and local levels. Presumably, undertakings aim, at least in part, at preserving or altering one or more situations in the United States or in the international system (or both) in ways thought by the officials to be consistent with the goals agreed on by them or by their predecessors.

This conception of the undertaking also makes the policy process sound more tidy than it really is. And it should be noted that it is still a porous definition. For example, the reference to action "primarily" by national executive and legislative branch officials and national, state, and local bureaucrats does not exclude either judicial officials at any level or state and local legislative officials. Nor does it exclude people who are not "duly constituted officials." In fact, in any individual instance of policy, any or all of the individuals not "primarily" involved in most undertakings may be critical figures. Also, it needs to be noted that the use of the word *goals* should not be taken to mean that those goals are necessarily present in clear, unambiguous, and widely agreed on form. In fact, goals of that character are exceedingly rare in the world of politics and policy in the United States.

Multiple Simultaneous Actors

The analyst of policy in the United States has to be keenly aware that any individual policy or program is likely to be dealt with simultaneously by a variety of actors from a number of different institutional homes. This fact, coupled with the fact that activities in several different stages can be going on at the same time, makes for a complex situation. Depending on one's degree of optimism about the susceptibility of such situations to analysis, the general situation might be described as either "rich" (the optimist speaks) or "confusing" (the pessimist's view). In any event, the analyst probably should have a simple two-dimensional matrix for trying to figure out what is happening at any given time. One dimension would be the different stages and the other dimension would be the major categories of actors. Not every cell is likely to be filled at any one time—although a number will be. And, over time, probably most of the cells will be filled. Figure 4.1 portrays this aid to organizing a beginning descriptive picture of what is happening in any policy area either at a single time or over time. How this type of matrix is used with regard to time depends on the form of the entries made in the cells. The matrix can be rather simple or can

Figure 4.1

A General Matrix for Use in Describing Policy Activities

Major Categories of Actors

Major Policy Process Stages	Executive Branch				Legislative Branch		Judicial Branch		Private Nongovernmental	
	National		State and Local		National	State and Local	National	State and Local	National	State and Local
	President and staff	Bureaucracy	Governor and staff; mayors	Bureaucracy	Congress	Elected assemblies	Courts	Courts	Groups	Groups
Agenda Building										
Formulation/ Legitimation										
Implementation										
Evaluation										
Decision about the Future										

become quite elaborate if subcategories of actors and functional activities as substages are used.

The Blurring of the Public-Private Line

The widespread affection for the validity and desirability of private activities and the suspicion of public (governmental) activities in the United States has meant that the line dividing government from nongovernment, in terms of both activities and personnel, is blurred. And it is easily crossed. Thus, individuals from the "private sector" are intimately involved in some governmental decisions in an informal sense. Statutes may provide that nongovernmental agencies are formally responsible for implementation of policy. A classic case involves state laws giving formal certification and licensing powers for various trades and professions to groups constituted of members of those trades or professions (barbers, river boat pilots, doctors, and so on).

"Privatization" has become a popular concept in recent years in the United States (and also in the United Kingdom). This involves formally moving what had been government enterprises (for example, mail service, phone service, garbage collection, or the Consolidated Rail Corporation in the United States or airlines or telecommunications in Great Britain) wholly or in part into the private sector in terms of both ownership and operational control. In the United States a lot of governmental activities have had some formal "privatization" for many years, and many more—probably most—have had some informal privatization. People, ideas, and influence move freely between the public and private sectors in the United States. (For an interesting discussion of some aspects of the continuum between public and private activities, see Dahl and Lindblom, 1953. For a contrast between traditional practices and attitudes in the United States and the United Kingdom, see King, 1973. However, attitudes in Reaganite America and Thatcherite Britain have drawn closer together at least at the level of national governmental officials.)

Channels of Access

Policy-making processes are relatively open to outside influence in the United States. The degree of openness is probably more widespread and more constant, particularly in terms of the bureaucracy, than it is in at least some other democratic countries. All democratic countries, by definition, have a number of elected officials, including legislators. Legislatures in democratic countries, again by definition, are open to representations of citizens, groups, and other parts of the public. In some democratic countries the bureaucracy may be relatively closed to outside influence. In the United States, however, the bureaucracy is thought to be properly open to outside influence (and I am not speaking of corrupt influence in the sense of bribery here). In the United States only the courts work within the limits of some expectation that they are not immediately open to the activities of lobbies of various sorts. (In fact, however, rather sophisticated lobbying efforts are made even in the case of the courts. They are also part of the fabric of political actors and preferences that lead to public policy, but not as immediately or evidently. In this volume, I concentrate on the executive and legislative branches, but the reader should not forget the political nature of the courts.)

We start, then, with the proposition (or perhaps it is simply a realization) that there is a presumption of penetrability or porousness about our legislative and executive/bureaucratic institutions. Officials in both branches can expect to receive the preferences of and accompanying pressure to act on those preferences from many different sources. Naturally, not all groups and individuals outside the government have the same degree of access. Who has what kind of access in what degree helps determine whose interests triumph when interests conflict.

It also needs to be stressed, however, that officials are not the passive recipients of outside pressures. They do not sit and wait for the public, interest groups, and influential

Figure 4.2

Channels of Access from the Public to Officials

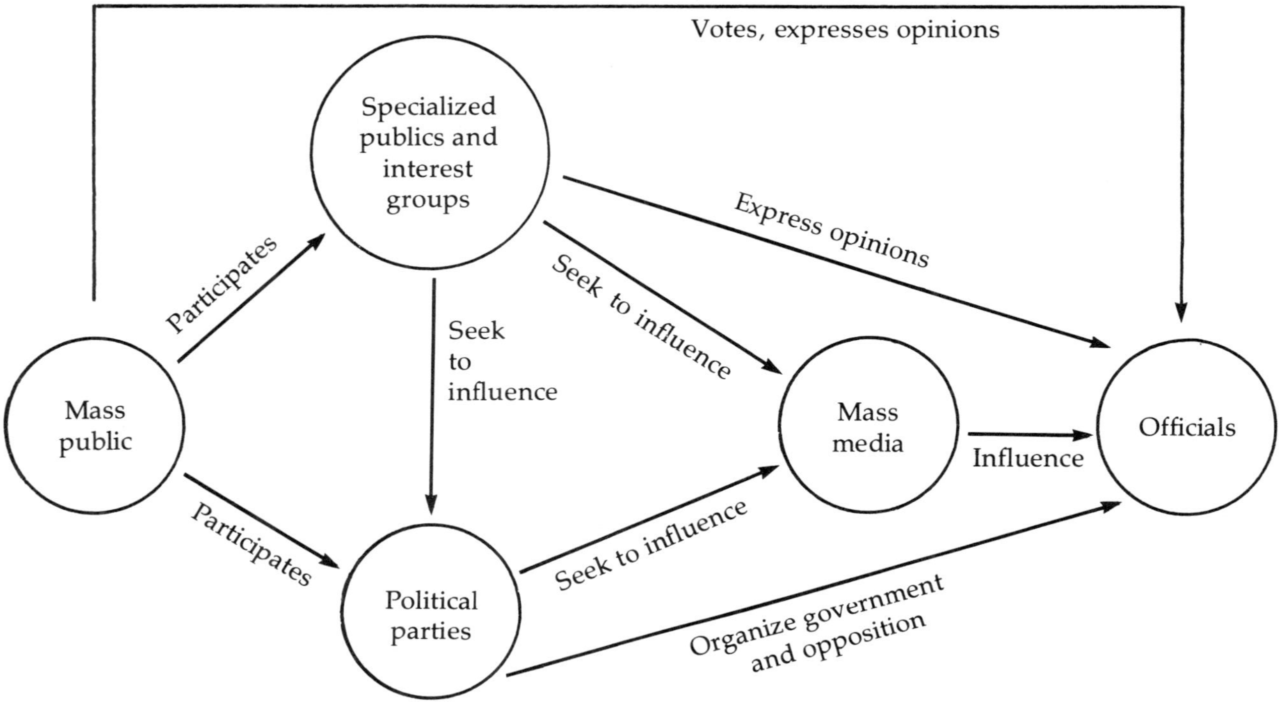

Figure 4.3

Channels of Access from Officials to the Public

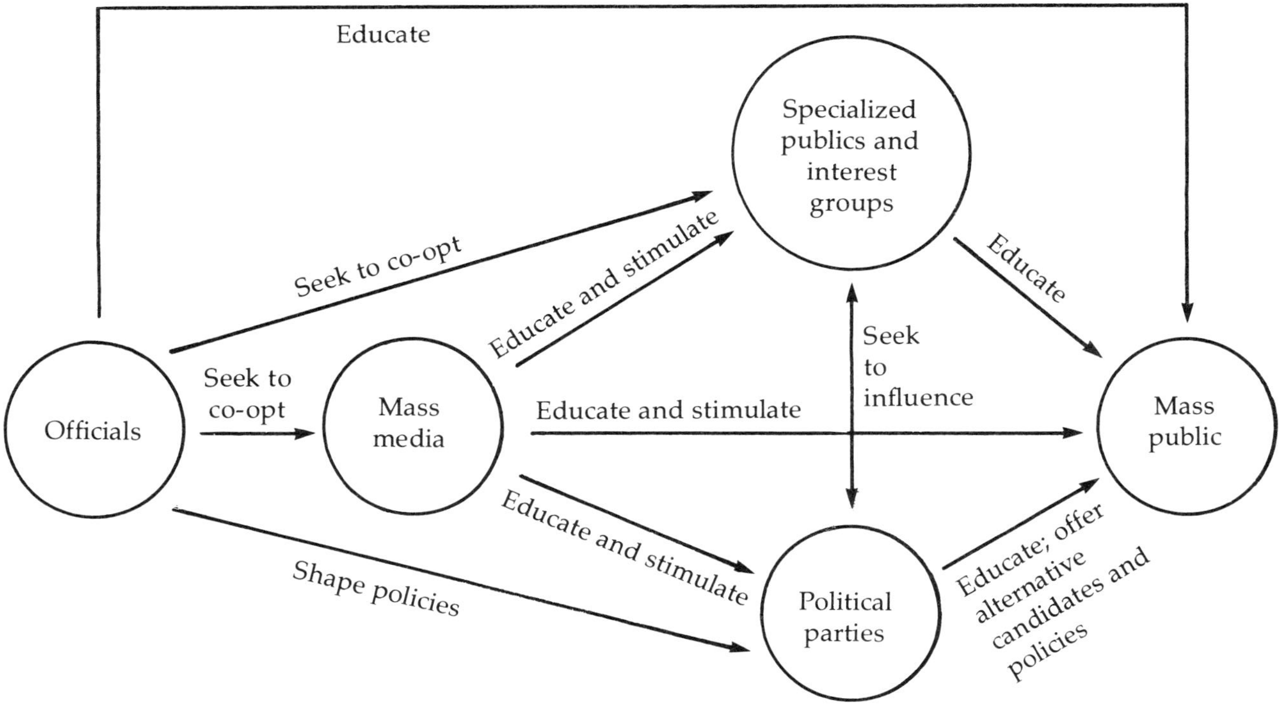

individuals to tell them what to do. They are not simply machines that register the mix of outside forces, preferences, and pressures they receive. Rather, the officials both in Congress and throughout the executive branch work to shape the preferences of various parts of the public. In short, the channels of access flow in both directions.

Figures 4.2 and 4.3 summarize the major channels of access between the public (in several forms) and officials (including legislative and executive/bureaucratic officials, both elected and unelected). The figures indicate two important points:

1. The concept of "the public" needs to be differentiated. For purposes of simplification, the distinction is made in the diagrams between the mass public and special publics and interest groups. More differentiations could be made and have been made by other analysts.

2. The public—virtually always in the form of specialized publics and interest groups—has some direct access to officials, and the officials have direct access in the other direction. However, influence in both directions is also mediated through two major sets of institutions: political parties and the mass media. In short, the transfer of opinions in either direction is usually a complex process involving many different actors.

The Nature of Agenda Building

Political scientists have paid only sporadic attention to agenda building as a policy phenomenon (for exceptions, see Cobb and Elder, 1983; Cobb, Ross, and Ross, 1976; Eyestone, 1978; Kingdon, 1984; Jones, 1984: ch. 4; and Bachrach and Baratz, 1962). I don't intend to present a theory of agenda building in elaborate fashion here. Some of the works cited develop such theories. Rather, I will offer some simplifications that relate to some of the theorizing that exists. The propositions embodying these simplifications follow and will be discussed individually.

1. The distinction between a public agenda and a formal agenda, although sometimes asserted to be universal, is applicable only to nondistributive and nonstructural policies.

2. Government officials are themselves often involved in agenda building. They do not merely process what someone else hands them or pressures them into thinking about. They can take one of four basic stances in relation to specific agenda items.

3. Three models of agenda building developed for cross-national comparison have considerable utility when adapted to the consideration of predominant agenda-building processes in different policy areas in the United States alone.

The Limited Utility of the Public Agenda/Formal Agenda Distinction

Most of the serious analyses of agenda building in the literature of political science make a distinction between a public (systemic) agenda and a formal (institutional or governmental or official) agenda. The public, or systemic, agenda is supposed to contain the major items about which large portions of society are concerned. The institutional, or governmental, agenda contains those items to which the government is currently paying attention. Merely paying attention, of course, does not guarantee action. Kingdon (1984:4) adds a useful additional category of a decision agenda: "the list of subjects within the governmental agenda that are up for an active decision."

Figure 4.4 is taken from Eyestone's study (1978) of social issues and summarizes his view of how problems become translated into issues and in turn into items on a public agenda and on an official agenda. Once they reach the status of official agenda items, they are candidates for

Figure 4.4

The Issue Translation Process in Ideal Form

			7. is placed on an official agenda	8. and a policy decision of some kind is made	9. groups may pursue a related issues strategy
		5. achieves a place on the public agenda			
	4. becomes a social issue		6. by the actions of issue entre-preneurs		or wait to try the same strategy in the next round
	(issue entre-preneurs are active here)				
		(more groups may join here)			
1. A social problem	3. is joined by groups with differing opinions				
2. perceived by groups					

Source: Robert Eyestone, *From Social Issues to Public Policy*, p. 104, Copyright © 1978, John Wiley & Sons, Inc. Reprinted by permission of John Wiley & Sons, Inc.

some action. Naturally, the policy decision to which item 8 in the figure refers may include a decision to do nothing.

The basic notion of the two agendas reflects the conclusion of the analysts that there are matters of concern to portions of the public that do not become the subjects of public action, at least for a long period of time. That is certainly the case some of the time. A number of people, both black and white, were concerned about the denial of civil rights to American blacks before the item was firmly on the governmental agenda. There was, for example, a gap of many decades between the founding of the National Association for the Advancement of Colored People in 1909 and the first hesitant federal government action (within the executive branch) on civil rights in the 1940s. Likewise, decades elapsed between the founding of the Urban League and the first, tentative governmental action in the 1940s. (See Kluger, 1976, for a thorough treatment of the development of the civil rights movement).

But there are other cases in which items come immediately onto the agenda. There simply is no separate "systemic" or "public" agenda in such cases. In terms of the typology developed in chapter 3, both distributive policy and structural policy fit this description. Interested parties in both kinds of policies come simultaneously from both the executive and legislative branches of the government (typically, one or more executive branch bureaus and one or more congressional subcommittees) and from the private sector (interest groups, corporations, unions). These subgovernments move items directly to the formal, or governmental, agenda because they do not need broader public support to get their items onto the agenda. In fact, they may not want public knowledge of what they seek because they fear that a more broadly informed portion of the public might oppose the distributive decisions that directly relate to their interests.

Even in other policy areas, matters may be put directly onto the governmental agenda without a period on a systemic agenda because government officials themselves are the principal agenda builders (see the discussion on this point in the next section). This is often the case with strategic policy (where the genuinely informed part of the public is quite small and governmental initiative is often necessary). Crisis situations, by definition, immediately put something onto the governmental agenda. Public discussion may take place over whether something is properly defined as a crisis, but that occurs only in a few cases (for example, the U.S. invasion of Grenada in 1983). In other cases (for example, Pearl Harbor in 1941 and the seizure of the American embassy in Iran in 1979), there is no discussion, and the fact of crisis is self-evident.

It is almost surely primarily in the areas of protective regulation and especially redistribution where the distinction between the systemic agenda and the governmental agenda makes the most sense, because the two agendas are most often genuinely distinguishable.

The Roles of Governmental Officials in Agenda Building

By definition, governmental officials are involved in determining the institutional agenda. But they also may be major participants in working toward putting something on the systemic agenda or, more likely, in short-circuiting the necessity for going through the systemic agenda before arriving on the governmental agenda.

Jones (1984: ch. 4) identifies three basic options and dismisses one that I would reinstate. The four options (the fourth is the reinstated one) follow. Government officials may take one of the following stances toward adding any individual item to the governmental agenda:

1. "Let it happen." In Jones' words, "government takes a relatively passive role in agenda setting. It maintains channels of access and communication so that those affected can be heard, but it does not reach out either to assist individuals and groups to define problems and organize or to assume the task of problem definition and priority setting."

2. "Encourage it to happen." Here, "the government reaches out to assist people in defining and articulating their problems. The bias of a totally free system toward the strong over the weak is acknowledged, and an effort is made to equalize resources so that the process of agenda setting does not favor one group or set of interests over another. Note that the emphasis here is in equipping people to participate—not in assuming the tasks of identifying and defining problems for them."

3. "Make it happen." In this case, "government plays an active role in defining problems and setting goals. Policy makers do not wait for the system to work; they direct its operations by establishing problem-defining and priority-setting mechanisms within government."

4. "Don't let it happen." In this option government not only does not help with problem definition and articulation but actually seeks to restrict or close the channels of access and communication. The government does not want to hear about problems in this area because it does not want these matters on the governmental agenda. (In an open society, of course, government cannot control the systemic agenda. In a closed society, government intervenes to prevent certain items from being discussed even in society and, in the most closed societies, to prescribe what must be discussed and what is, therefore, on the systemic agenda.)

Three Types of Agenda Building for Different Types of Policy

Cobb, Ross, and Ross (1976) attempted to look at agenda building in a cross-national sense. They produced three models of agenda building in that context that also have some utility for considering agenda building in the area of domestic policy within the United States. Two of the models seem particularly likely to be useful in understanding two of the major categories of domestic policy. The link of the third one to a particular type of policy is much less clear.

Cobb, Ross, and Ross call their three types of agenda building outside initiative, mobilization, and inside access.

The first model—outside initiative—"applies to the situation in which a group outside the government structure (1) articulates a grievance, (2) tries to expand interest in the issue to enough other groups in the population to gain a place on the public agenda, in order to (3) create sufficient pressure on decision makers to force the issue onto the formal agenda for their serious consideration" (p. 132). In the United States this is often (although not always) how redistributive issues are treated (using the peculiarly unidirectional American definition of redistributive as involving only policies that are perceived to generate redistribution from the more well-off to the less well-off).

The second model—inside access—"describes a pattern of agenda building and policy formation which attempts to exclude the participation of the public. Proposals arise within governmental units or in groups close to the government" (p. 136). This model would certainly be overwhelmingly predominant in setting the governmental agenda in the distributive area. The clusters of people (subgovernments) dominating policy when it is distributive want to control agenda building as well as all other aspects of policy formulation, implementation, and evaluation. When some other form of agenda setting is used, it is a sign that the ruling subgovernment is at least under attack and may be in some trouble in terms of perpetuating its exclusive favored position.

The third model—mobilization—"describes the process of agenda building in situations where political leaders initiate a policy, but require the support of the mass public for its implementation." This is a model that is used in a minority of redistributive policies and is used with some frequency (although certainly not exclusively) in protective regulatory policies. The "mass public" referred to in the definition may really be a specialized public in some instances.

Influence in Formulation and Legitimation

Figures 4.5 through 4.10 summarize the patterns of interaction and influence in the typical formulation and legitimation policy making in the six policy areas discussed in chapter 3. These visual summaries identify the principal actors, and they suggest the relative importance of different channels of interaction and the direction of the influence one set of actors has over another. Obviously, these diagrams simplify reality. But such simplification, after all, is the job of the analyst. The patterns for distributive policy and structural policy are identical. Each of the other four is partially unique.

A Few Recent Cases: Agenda Building, Formulation, and Legitimation Politics Illustrated

In order to "prove" the accuracy of a lot of the assertions, conclusions, and hypotheses in this chapter and in chapter 3, a vast amount of data and analysis would be needed. The collection, analysis, and presentation of such findings are well beyond the scope of this volume. Some evidence is present in other sources (on the utility of the basic policy typology in distinguishing different political patterns, for example, see Ripley and Franklin, 1984, on formulation and legitimation, and Ripley and Franklin, 1982, on implementation). As yet, there is no definitive work or set of works aggregating all of the evidence that would be needed for a comprehensive test. Such aggregation represents a major research agenda for a number of scholars. And some have set off to research various parts of suggestions contained in this book.

In order to illustrate *some* of the complexities and *some* of the patterns in policy making that have been analyzed

Figure 4.5

Relative Importance of Relationships for Determining Distributive Policy

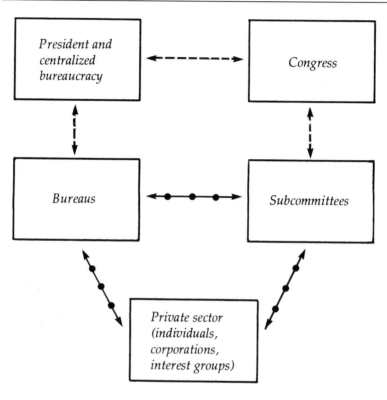

Key:

⬤—⬤—⬤ – *very important relationship*

———— – *moderately important relationship*

— — — — – *relatively unimportant relationship*

Lack of an arrow indicates a relationship that occurs only rarely

Source: Randall B. Ripley and Grace A. Franklin, *Congress, the Bureaucracy, and Public Policy*, 3rd ed. © Dorsey Press, 1984, p. 239.

Figure 4.6

Relative Importance of Relationships for Determining Protective Regulatory Policy

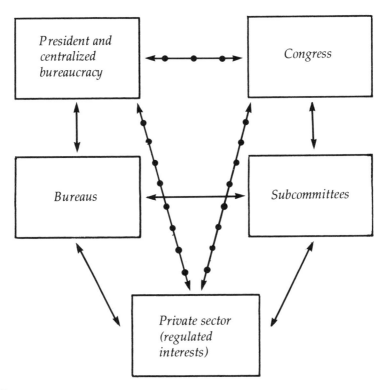

Key:

—●—●— — very important relationship

————— — moderately important relationship

------- — relatively unimportant relationship

Lack of an arrow indicates a relationship that occurs only rarely

Source: Randall B. Ripley and Grace A. Franklin, *Congress, the Bureaucracy, and Public Policy*, 3rd ed. © Dorsey Press, 1984, p. 240.

Figure 4.7

Relative Importance of Relationships for Determining Redistributive Policy

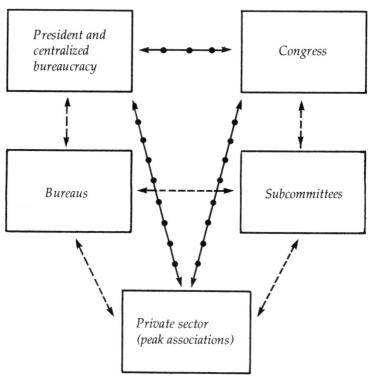

Key:

——●——●—— – *very important relationship*

————— – *moderately important relationship*

— — — – *relatively unimportant relationship*

Lack of an arrow indicates a relationship that occurs only rarely

Source: Randall B. Ripley and Grace A. Franklin, *Congress, the Bureaucracy, and Public Policy*, 3rd ed. © Dorsey Press, 1984, p. 241.

Figure 4.8

Relative Importance of Relationships for Determining Structural Policy

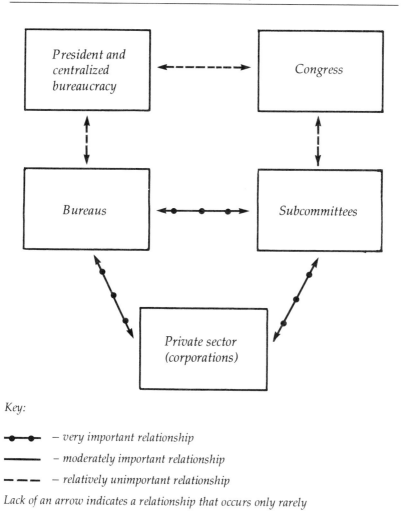

Key:

●━━●━━ – *very important relationship*

━━━━━ – *moderately important relationship*

━ ━ ━ – *relatively unimportant relationship*

Lack of an arrow indicates a relationship that occurs only rarely

Source: Randall B. Ripley and Grace A. Franklin, *Congress, the Bureaucracy, and Public Policy,* 3rd ed. © Dorsey Press, 1984, p. 242.

Figure 4.9

Relative Importance of Relationships for Determining Strategic Policy

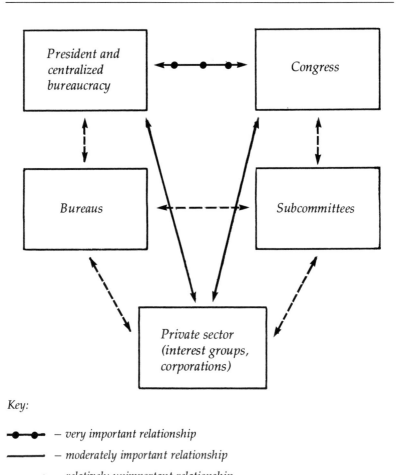

Key:

—●—●— – very important relationship

———— – moderately important relationship

— — — – relatively unimportant relationship

Lack of an arrow indicates a relationship that occurs only rarely

Source: Randall B. Ripley and Grace A. Franklin, *Congress, the Bureaucracy, and Public Policy*, 3rd ed. © Dorsey Press, 1984, p. 243.

Figure 4.10

Relative Importance of Relationships for Determining Crisis Policy

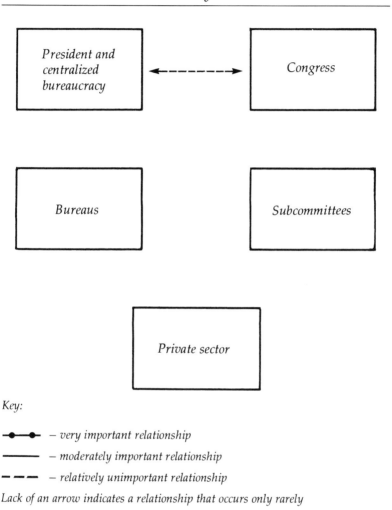

Key:

●—●— – *very important relationship*

——— – *moderately important relationship*

— — — – *relatively unimportant relationship*

Lack of an arrow indicates a relationship that occurs only rarely

Source: Randall B. Ripley and Grace A. Franklin, *Congress, the Bureaucracy, and Public Policy*, 3rd. ed. © Dorsey Press, 1984, p. 244.

abstractly so far, it seems worthwhile to present a few brief examples. I have chosen three recent policies in the domestic area of U.S. policy and will present a few basic facts about them and offer a few interpretative comments. For each policy I will first present a basic chronology of developments in recent years. Then I will discuss the agenda building and formulation and legitimation processes with regard to each of the three cases, making comments as I go. Additional sections on implementation in each of the same three policy areas will appear in chapter 5.

The cases fall, one each, into the distributive, protective regulatory, and redistributive categories. Such an array, of course, offers no "proof" of anything comparative, but I want the reader to have a rough feel for a major example of policy of each type.

Water Resources: Distributive Policy

Water resources have been a major distributive policy area in the United States. As a symbol of the potency of the subject it is worth noting that even President Reagan moderated his critical attitude toward water projects just before he formally kicked off his re-election campaign in early 1984 as a way of solidifying his political base in the western part of the United States (see *Washington Post,* Jan. 25, 1984).

General Chronology. Federal involvement in development of the nation's water resources has had a long and rich history. Once started, this form of distributive policy has proved immensely popular. The initial reason for the involvement was to help stimulate the new nation's economic development. The first Rivers and Harbors bill was passed in 1824 (it provided for improving the navigability of the Ohio River). The Army Corps of Engineers (ACE) had been established a little over twenty years before and was given responsibility for this project and for subsequent ones. Rivers and Harbors legislation has emerged regularly from

Congress since 1824. The number of projects, level of funding, purposes served, and groups of beneficiaries have all increased dramatically.

In 1902, the Reclamation Act established the Bureau of Reclamation (BR) and made it responsible for recovering arid land and developing water sources in seventeen western states. The act set a limit of 160 acres per farmer on the amount of land that could receive federally subsidized irrigation water. In practice this limit has been ignored, to the benefit of large agribusiness corporations in California and Arizona. A strong rivalry between ACE and BR developed because both agencies had overlapping responsibilities and jurisdictions.

The passage of the Boulder Canyon Act in 1928 authorized the BR to begin construction of Hoover Dam. This was the first of several major new dams to be built. The law also contained for the first time a policy statement endorsing the concept that water projects should serve multiple purposes (such as navigation, generation of power, recreation, irrigation, conservation).

The 1936 Flood Control Act was a landmark piece of legislation. The federal government assumed responsibility for controlling flooding in all of the river basins in the country. The ACE was given responsibility for implementation. Multiuse projects were the goal, and the pattern of continual congressional involvement in decisions about projects to be chosen was formalized.

From 1940 to the present, booming population growth in the Southwest has led to demands from that area of the country for more water to support the needs of cities, industries, and agriculture. Competition between states for shares of river water has been intense, but the Arizona-California battle over the Colorado River has been the most heated of all. Since 1922 those states have contested their "fair" shares. Legislation introduced in 1949–51 to give Arizona a larger portion was defeated. The issue was litigated between 1952 and 1963, when the Supreme Court found in favor of Arizona. The Central Arizona Project, authorized by Congress in 1968, launched a huge project to divert a portion of the Colorado to central Arizona.

Continued jockeying between administration officials, Office of Management and Budget officials, and Congress over the relative influence of each in decisions about water projects has also marked the post-1945 period. Presidents since Truman have tried to decrease congressional control, tighten selection criteria, cut costs, and increase benefits, but until the late 1970s, their impact was not discernible. Congress remained the dominant partner.

From 1976 to the present, Presidents Carter and Reagan have begun to chip away at the classic pork barrel nature of water project decision making. They have been aided by a growing national deficit. Carter's dramatic, though less than effective, attack on water projects in 1977 raised the visibility of decision-making routines to a national level. Carter's water reform policies were not enacted, but did have incremental effect on decision making. The Reagan administration continued to advocate cost sharing for states receiving water projects (whereby recipients would have to help finance the projects). No new projects for ACE were authorized by Congress in this period. The Reagan administration may have opened the floodgates to new activity with its 1984 election-related reversal of some key policies.

A recent decision of some importance was the 1982 revision of the 1902 Reclamation Act. Congress increased the amount of land that could be watered by federally subsidized water. Charges to users for the water provided were kept well below the actual cost of producing the water. The huge agricultural firms with thousands of acres were not disturbed by the final legislation; the 1902 rhetoric of water for the small family farmer was ignored in the final outcome. The votes in both houses were decisive.

Agenda Building. Water projects have been on the governmental agenda continuously since the 1820s. Initially, federal involvement was prompted by the need to improve navigation and thereby commerce and communication. This form of nation building via public works had the politically attractive side effect of allowing projects to be spread around the country. Quickly, the pork barrel character of water projects was established. Water issues remained on the government agenda in a secure position of low visibility.

Occasionally external events have brought water issues to public attention. One such occasion was flooding in the 1920s and 1930s, which led to expanded governmentally subsidized flood control projects (the 1936 Flood Control Act). Water was on the agenda after World War II, when mushrooming population growth in the arid states of the Southwest led to greatly increased demand for the vital liquid resource. Interstate competition for water in the Southwest was settled in the courts and took the form of a huge water diversion program (1968 Central Arizona Project) and increased acreage limits (1982 Reclamation Act). President Carter mounted a highly visible but poorly orchestrated attack on pork barrel water projects in 1977 that temporarily disturbed the routine handling of water projects.

Most of the time water development issues are not on a public or social agenda but are continuously on the governmental agenda. When they do come to public attention, it is usually for a relatively short period of time.

Formulation and Legitimation. The general pattern of formulation and legitimation for water resources is that of classic distributive decision making: agreement among members of the subgovernment is high; proceedings have low public visibility; membership in subgovernments is stable; ratification by House and Senate full committees and full houses is routine; and the influence of subgovernments in shaping the final outcome is very high. Support for water projects comes from a wide array of beneficiaries. The multiple purposes strategy discussed above broadens the base of support and enhances the logroll mode of policy formulation and legitimation.

Subgovernments form around both the ACE and BR. Local interest groups representing construction, transportation, power users, conservationists, recreation interests, and others join forces with members of subcommittees in the House and Senate (from the Public Works and Interior and Insular Affairs committees) and with bureaucrats from the ACE and BR. Normal operation of both subgovernments is similar. Formulation and legitimation involves a two-step procedure. First, project feasibility is determined through a piece of legislation requesting a feasibility study to be conducted by the agency. The level of local interest at this stage is already high since the proposal originates at the local level. Second, bureaucrats and subcommittee members determine which of the feasible projects ought to be authorized, and these recommendations are embodied in an authorization bill. Typically the authorization bill is hammered out in the subcommittee and ratified by the full committees and entire Congress without debate.

This pattern has been disrupted when external events force water issues into sustained public prominence. Visibility increases participation from actors outside the subgovernment. The main intrusive actor is usually the president or his agent, the Office of Management and Budget. Their intervention is aimed at imposing greater executive control over assessment of feasibility and selection criteria for projects. Carter's role in 1977–80 was significant because, even though he achieved less than half of what he wanted, he nonetheless achieved more than previous presidents. He did veto a major Public Works bill in 1978 because it included funding for water projects that he didn't want, and Congress sustained the veto.

Members of Congress other than subcommittee members also get personally involved in decision making when the level of controversy and visibility rise and when regional stakes are high. For example, in the debate over the authorization of the Central Arizona Project, senators and representatives from the Northwest were successful in opposing proposals to divert water from rivers in the Northwest to the Southwest to help relieve the pressure on the Colorado River.

Table 4.1

The Federal Role in Strip-Mining Regulation: A Chronology

1967	President Johnson sends a Department of Interior study on surface mining to Congress. The study recommends development of nationwide federal standards for strip-mining reclamation practices.
1968	An administration bill is submitted (Surface Mining Reclamation Act); a Senate Interior subcommittee holds hearings on this and two other Senate bills. No other legislative action is taken.
1969–71	No action.
1972	The House passes a strip-mining regulation bill, but the Senate does not act.
1973	The Senate passes a bill, but the House fails to act.
1974	Both houses overwhelmingly pass a strip-mine regulation bill, but President Ford uses the pocket veto to kill it.
1975	Within six months, the bill passes again in both houses, but President Ford vetos it, and the veto is sustained in the House by three votes.
1976	The House Rules Committee prevents the bill from coming to the floor because the president is hostile to the bill.
1977	President Carter endorses a surface mining law. House and Senate pass a slightly weaker version than the 1975 bill, which becomes law as the Surface Mining Control and Reclamation Act of 1977.
1978–81	Multiple court cases are brought against the new law by states and mining companies seeking relief from the law and the regulations drafted by Interior. In June 1981, the Supreme Court declares the law to be constitutional.
1981–83	Secretary of Interior Watt uses administrative and budget actions to weaken regulations and redirect implementation from the federal to state level. Very limited enforcement activity by the federal government occurs under Watt.

Strip-Mining Regulation: Protective Regulatory Policy

Unlike water resources, the role of the federal government in regulating strip mining is very new. Presidential endorsement of a federal role in this area came only in 1968, and the basic statute was passed in 1977. Table 4.1 summarizes the most salient features of the chronology from 1967 through 1983.

Agenda Building. The environmental movement was a significant factor in general in the 1960s and 1970s and was important in putting strip-mining regulation on the societal agenda in that period. The environmentalists focused public attention on a host of environmental issues, including clean air and water, energy conservation, and reclamation of land that had been strip mined.

In the mining areas of the eastern United States, where strip mining has gone on for decades, the devastation of the unreclaimed mine sites was obvious to residents, tourists, and politicians, although they tended to be relatively complacent about the situation. No single factor explains how public consciousness about the scars left by strip mining was transmitted onto a governmental agenda. Certainly the publicity surrounding the first "Earth Day" in 1970 created a broad public awareness of environmental issues in general, and environmental lobbyists worked assiduously and with increasing political sophistication to obtain legislation to conserve and preserve nonrenewable natural resources. In the 1970s also, the "energy crisis" provoked multiple and uncoordinated governmental attempts to develop nonfossil fuels and to regulate existing sources of energy. Coal was and is an important alternative source of energy in abundant supply in this country.

Formulation and Legitimation. It took nine years to produce a law to regulate strip mining. The opening salvo was a report prepared by the Department of the Interior recommending a national policy and national standards for reclamation and strip mining. The first bill was submitted by President Johnson in 1968, but serious congressional attention did not begin until 1972. Simultaneous support in both houses was absent until 1974. In 1974 and 1975, a president hostile to regulation of coal mining twice vetoed legislation passed by both houses. In 1976, fearful of another veto and unable to override it, house and senate leadership withheld bills from floor consideration. In the period up to 1977, the central issue for debate was whether there would be any federal regulation at all, and if so, how much and what kind.

By 1977, a new president supportive of environmental legislation in general and of strip mining regulation in particular, provided important leadership. A majority in both House and Senate still favored the legislation, and passage was secure. The law that emerged was somewhat weaker than previous versions passed in earlier years, reflecting serious compromises between proregulation forces and antiregulation forces. As occurred in earlier years, final decisions about the content of the law were made on the floor of House and Senate in substantive amendments, not in the quiet of subcommittee deliberations. The proregulation group limited the focus of the bill to coal mining, because they recognized that a bill that encompassed all mining activity would not pass. The coal industry, which accounts for the bulk of strip mining, saw the writing on the wall and worked to amend the bill rather than to defeat it. They secured a variety of concessions, exemptions, and delays. But the final product was not a limp or purely symbolic piece of legislation. It established federal standards for reclamation and required states to meet environmental standards. The coal companies, especially those in the eastern United States, were greatly displeased with the law. Western operators felt it would be somewhat easier for them to comply and were less hostile. The industry in general, however, has continued to oppose strict implementation after 1977.

Employment and Training: Redistributive Policy

General Chronology. The principal pieces of legislation marking the history of the federal involvement in providing employment and training programs for those generally disadvantaged in the labor market are the act establishing the Civilian Conservation Corps (1933); the Manpower Development and Training Act (1962); the Equal Opportunity Act (1964); the Comprehensive Employment and Training Act (CETA) (1973); the Emergency Jobs Program added as a separate title to CETA in 1974; a youth title for CETA (1977); CETA reauthorization and amendments (1978), which included the addition of a separate title providing for a Private Sector Initiative Program; and the Job Training Partnership Act (1982), which is the replacement for CETA and represents the current federal involvement in this redistributive area.

Employment and training legislation existed in the 1930s, but it focused on public employment programs, not training. The Civilian Conservation Corps and Works Progress Administration were responses to the magnitude of unemployment that cut across most classes in society. Programs were also a response to the direct leadership and proposals of the president. Federal attention to employment and training lapsed after the Depression.

In the 1960s, a variety of actors in the nongovernmental arena pushed employment and training programs back onto the governmental agenda. Aggregate unemployment (the kind that affects all classes of people) was creeping upward. New kinds of unemployment were being discovered: unemployment for certain groups of people—the poor and minorities—was way above average, and technological unemployment was making a debut. People out of work because of automation needed to be retrained. Awareness of the poverty problem in America was growing. The civil rights movement among black Americans stressed the need for political and economic opportunity. Finally, violent urban riots in the 1960s sparked both fear and some sense of social conscience.

The president's Great Society proposals were a leading influence in shaping legislative proposals, and congressional committees were principal actors in establishing federal programs for employment and training.

Employment and training programs stayed on the governmental agenda after the 1960s through interaction of congressional committees and subcommittees, interest groups, and the administration. The 1962 and 1964 laws were frequently amended to change recipients, administrative patterns, and funding levels. Programs operating under MDTA (1962) and EOA (1964) were initially targeted to different client groups, but over time, all programs except the MDTA on the job-training program focused on the unemployed and the economically disadvantaged. MDTA and EOA programs were alike in their principal features of implementation. They produced a large number of separate categorical grant programs with a dynamic federal presence (in the form of strong leadership from federal departments and persistent congressional oversight). They proliferated the number of service delivery agencies at the local level, where programs and service to beneficiaries were uncoordinated. EOA and its administrative agency, the Office of Economic Opportunity, continually faced the hostility of a significant segment of Congress. EOA underwent almost annual reauthorizations, and its programs were gradually diluted, given away to other agencies, or deleted.

As part of his New Federalism campaign, President Nixon helped push through reform of manpower legislation (CETA) in 1973. The CETA compromise required over four years of negotiations with congressional committees. Its principal features were partial consolidation of many of the fragmented programs of EOA and MDTA and a decentralization of administrative responsibility to local units of government. Congressional committees and subcommittees for Labor and Human Resources in the Senate and Education and Labor in the House were equal partners with the president in shaping the CETA legislation. The inclusion of a small public employment program was a significant compromise by the president.

In 1974, unemployment rose quickly, and Congress, with President Ford's assent, added a new title to CETA to combat unemployment through a program of locally administered public employment jobs. In 1975, amendments to client eligibility addressed the growing problem of a lessening of service to the most disadvantaged, especially in the public employment titles of CETA. In 1978, a small but significant role was mandated for the private sector in addressing local employment and training programs.

In the late 1970s and early 1980s, disenchantment was widespread with CETA's accomplishments. Though evaluations of program performance and effectiveness had been conducted throughout CETA's implementation, results were slow in coming and poorly communicated to politicians. Some abuses in public employment programs created a public belief /that all CETA programs were bad. In the setting of inconclusive results poorly presented, President Reagan's assertive and ideologically based leadership toward a new, much narrower vision of federal employment and training programs was persuasive. JTPA maintained a decentralized approach, but changed local municipalities for state governments as principal administrative agencies. The federal role was almost eliminated, and the private sector role was increased. Although unemployment remained high, the president successfully rejected public service employment as an employment and training tool. Instead, he promoted a small retraining program for unemployed workers that was reminiscent of the 1962 MDTA program.

Agenda Building. In the late 1960s, a confluence of highly visible social events directed societal attention to the need for remedial employment and training programs. Concern with racial equality (political and economic) grew as the Civil Rights movement in the South developed. Urban riots were prevalent in the mid 1960s. Poverty was "discovered" by academics. The cycle of poverty was hypothesized to imprison people in an inescapable condition of poor education, poor or no employment, and high crime. Aggregate unemployment rose after the Korean War. Fear of the economic effects of automation and technological unemployment grew. The urban riots cemented a commitment to do something, if for no other reason than to damp down the fires of violence.

In the 1980s, public concern for remedial programs waned, despite evidence that poverty was still a widespread problem and that unemployment among minorities and the poor was still higher than average. The decline in public concern was linked to statements by the president that poverty was no longer a problem and that, even if it were, the private sector or states and localities, rather than the federal government, ought to be dealing with it. After twenty years of federal programs, poverty certainly had not been eradicated. Reagan concluded that the government was, therefore, ineffective and should quit trying to help very much except for providing what he called a "safety net." Most Americans did not object when employment and training and other poverty programs were cut back.

The transfer of social concerns to a governmental agenda occurred relatively quickly in the 1960s (the speed became apparent when compared to some other redistributive programs like voting rights and Medicaid). Employment and training programs entered the governmental agenda as part of a larger package of Great Society proposals initiated by President Johnson in the wake of President Kennedy's assassination. With huge Democratic majorities in both houses, Johnson's proposal for a War on Poverty swept through Congress. The president's plan to eliminate poverty included multiple employment and training programs. Despite disagreements, employment and training programs have remained on the federal government agenda since 1962.

Formulation and Legitimation. The shaping of the CETA bill in 1973 was a product of four years of attempts to fashion a manpower reform bill. The primary aims were to reduce fragmentation of programs at the local level by transferring control for planning and administration from the federal government to local governments. Much debate centered on the role of public employment programs in the reform bill. The president and both houses of Congress were active in the four year period in initiating proposals. Two major efforts occurred, one in 1970, which produced a compromise bill that the president subsequently vetoed (for its inclusion of public service jobs and lack of decategorization), and the second in 1973. Bitterness over the 1970 veto dampened congressional interest in 1971 and 1972, but Congress did pass a small public service employment bill in 1972 that Nixon signed (the program was small, unemployment was rising and thus it was politically popular, and eligibility for participants was open ended). In 1973, both House and Senate worked seriously with the administration to shape a bill acceptable to principal opposing coalitions and to the president. A spirit of compromise prevailed.

Most parties got something in the final passage. The president and conservatives got decentralization to the local level and decategorization of what were then called manpower programs. But they had to accept public service employment (PSE). Liberals and Democrats got PSE but had to accept a lessening of federal involvement in program planning and implementation. Municipalities got administrative responsibility, but comprehensiveness of the legislation was limited, and not all manpower programs were included.

The interests most heavily represented in passage of both CETA and JTPA were those of administrative units— local and federal governments in the case of CETA and state governments and private industry councils in JTPA. The main battles were fought over how much and what kind of decentralization would occur. Disagreements about eligibility of clients were most often resolved by broadening the pool of beneficiaries. In 1982, JTPA defined eligibility narrowly to concentrate on welfare recipients and disadvantaged youth, but living stipends were also eliminated, raising serious doubts about whether disadvantaged persons could afford to participate.

Summary

1. Although it is analytically useful to conceive of the policy process in terms of stages, it is also important to understand the complex interrelated nature of those stages through an integrating concept, here called the "undertaking."

2. Policy-making processes in the United States are porous: they are open to many outside influences. They also involve simultaneously many actors with different institutional affiliations.

3. Agenda building is a complex and somewhat murky process, but systematic attention to it is vital, since it starts the policy process in several senses. Agenda building is not a single process in society. Rather, it is a set of processes in both society and the government. Government officials do not simply wait for an agenda to be presented to them; instead, they engage in a number of important agenda-building activities themselves.

4. There are predictable patterns of relationships between key actors that vary by policy type. Different types of policy tend to be decided by predictable configurations of institutional actors.

5

The Nature and Evaluation of Implementation

In this chapter and the next, the focus is on the evaluative character of the study of implementation (chapter 5) and impact (chapter 6). In the preceding chapter I dealt with areas of the policy process—agenda building, formulation, and legitimation—that in recent decades have involved only minimal evaluative efforts by political scientists. Most studies are a combination of description and analysis. These studies attempt to explain what happens and why. In the area of agenda building there are relatively few studies, and they tend to be general—"nomothetic" as the jargon would have it. In the area of formulation and legitimation there are lots of studies, and a large proportion of them tend to be case studies—"idiographic" in the jargon.

The areas of policy and program implementation and impact are more obviously subject to evaluation than the areas dealt with in chapter 4, at least in the way they have been treated in recent years by political scientists who have worked on them. There have also been some studies simply describing and analyzing processes, especially in the area of implementation, but a number of implementation studies are evaluative, and virtually all impact studies are evaluative. There could also be descriptive/analytic studies to figure out what happened and why in terms of impact, but few impact studies seek to stop without making a judgment, either explicit or implicit, about the relative goodness or badness of the outcome. There could also be a number of studies asking about the utilization of policy research, but, in fact, there are only a few empirical studies about utilization, in part because there is no widespread agreement on the meaning of utilization. I will return to the theme of utilization at the end of chapter 6.

Table 5.1 summarizes an impressionistic picture of the literature of political science dealing with the four major stages of the policy process: agenda building, formulation

Table 5.1

Type and Relative Number of Studies in Political Science Policy Literature

Policy Stage	Relative Number of Studies, by Type	
	Descriptive/ Analytic Studies	Evaluative Studies
Agenda Building	Few	Very few
Formulation, Legitimation	Many; mostly case studies	Few
Implementation	Some	Some; focus is on specific programs
Impact	Few	Some; focus is on specific programs

and legitimation, implementation, and impact. The two columns divide the studies that have been done focusing on each stage into those that are primarily descriptive and analytic ("disciplinary" might be an appropriate synonym) and those that are primarily evaluative ("judgmental," usually including recommendations of some sort about how to improve the situation analyzed and evaluated). Naturally, good evaluative studies are based on solid description and analysis. And there may be at least some implicit evaluation in studies that attempt to be solely descriptive and analytic.

The table suggests, as was said at the outset of chapter 4, that the bread and butter of policy studies (not policy analysis as used in this book and laid out in chapter 1) is descriptive/analytic studies of formulation and legitimation, often (although not exclusively by any means) in the form of case studies. At this point the table is presented merely to suggest the general shape of the literature. In chapter 7, I will return to this gross assessment of the state of the literature when I discuss the best and most important contributions political scientists can make to policy analysis.

Chapter 2 defined, very briefly, the implementation and impact stages. Chapter 3 applied the basic policy typology for the domestic arena to implementation. In this chapter and the next I will continue to explore implementation and impact by pursuing specific topics.

In chapter 5, topics were chosen to deal a bit more (beyond chapter 3) with the empirical dimension of implementation and with the kind of good analysis that seems feasible for political scientists to undertake. Thus the rest of the present chapter will first deal with the nature of the evaluation of implementation. Then it will deal briefly with the patterns of interaction and influence hypothesized to exist in implementation. The chapter will end with a brief summary of implementation events in the same domestic policy areas used to illustrate formulation and legitimation in chapter 4: water resources, strip-mining regulation, and employment and training.

In chapter 6, after some brief introductory considerations, I will discuss (1) designing and conducting formative evaluations of social programs (which evaluations blend a study of implementation with a study of at least short-run impacts); (2) the meaning of impact; and (3) the utilization of analysis and evaluation.

The Evaluation of Implementation

Two Perspectives

Implementation studies have two major foci: "compliance" and "what's happening?" The first stream of studies, emerging from a tradition of concerns in the literature of public administration, is focused primarily on questions of compliance. These studies view agencies and the people in those agencies as functioning within the confines of hierarchical arrangements. In this view, there are definite superiors and subordinates in terms of both bureaucratic units and individual bureaucrats.

The questions developed in an implementation study of this character have to do with whether subordinate agencies and individuals obey superior agencies and individuals. The assumption is made that if the degree of obedience to the wishes of superiors is high, "good" implementation will take place. "Bad" implementation occurs when subordinates behave insubordinately rather than faithfully following the directives of superiors. "Bad" implementation can also result if the superiors give unclear instructions.

At its best (see, for example, Kaufman, 1960 and 1973) this kind of analysis is rich in the political analysis of organizational behavior. On the other hand, programs are not analyzed in their own right but rather as artifacts stemming from the character and quality of organizational behavior. The assumption is that if the bureaucratic relationships are in order programs will generally work.

At least two major comments on deficiencies in this view are in order. First, many nonbureaucratic influences are likely to be at work in determining what any given layer of bureaucracy can achieve. Second, some programs are so maldesigned that perfect bureaucratic behavior, obedience, and coordination may still produce a program that appears to be badly implemented because it is not working.

These comments raise a question about the meaning of implementation and "success" in implementation. Is "successful" implementation simply that in which superior bureaucrats issue clear orders and inferior bureaucratics behave in accordance with them? That may well mark a "successful" bureaucratic organization of a certain type, although some would certainly argue that neither in empirical nor in normative terms is that the way bureaucracy behaves or should behave (see, for example, Lindblom, 1965).

Alternatively, is "successful" implementation "that which facilitates desired program performance and impact" (Ripley and Franklin, 1982: 204)? If that is the case the role of implementation in helping produce desired results, both short-term and long-term, needs to be assessed. By definition, of course, implementation activities on the part of bureaucrats are only part of the activities and events that help determine the degree or amount of desired results that occur. In this conception "successful" implementation is tied only to "successful" programs. Yet it may well take a long period of time to judge the nature and degree of success in the programs themselves. And, of course, lots of factors, ranging from program design to a variety of external events and forces, impinge on the degree of programmatic success.

Some compliance perspective studies get outside of a single bureaucracy and realize that compliance is a complicated phenomenon involving, typically, several bureaucracies with a mix of federal headquarters, federal field offices, and various state and local bureaucracies. In such a study there is even room for examining the "compliance" of non-governmental units. (For a good early statement along these lines, see Van Meter and Van Horn, 1975a. Note that Van Horn's subsequent work has evolved more in the direction of the "what's happening?" perspective, discussed next. See Van Horn and Van Meter, 1976, and, especially, Van Horn, 1979.)

The diagrams in figure 5.1 portray the two major compliance variants of the relationships that are of interest in an implementation study coming from the compliance perspective. Part A of the figure displays a simple hierarchical model of a single agency. The assumption is that the state of relations between the superior and subordinate units constitute the most important variables in determining the nature of implementation activities. Part B of the figure suggests a more complex set of interbureaucratic relations that leaves room for different agencies at several territorial levels and nongovernmental organizations and actors to be involved in ways that are central to determining what is going on in terms of implementation. The concept of "compliance" in the case of the complex situation simply portrayed in Part B of figure 5.1 is much more sophisticated than that in the case of Part A. And concern for compliance begins to be one of many concerns, although still the principal concern.

These comments lead us to the second perspective, which is very different from the compliance perspective. It can best be described, though somewhat inelegantly, as a "what's happening?" perspective. A study of implementation of this character is likely to be an investigation that implies a linear model of antecedents of various kinds (many of them political) of implementation and consequences of different types. A concern with compliance and with conditions fostering it or working against it (for example, bureaucratic resources or implementers' preferences) is considered part of the concerns about the implementation phase itself. Figure 5.2 portrays the typical linear model that motivates this kind of research.

Figure 5.1

Relationships of Interest in Two Types of Compliance Implementation Studies

Nature of Participants

(arrows indicate relationships to be explored)

Part A: A Single Agency (A)

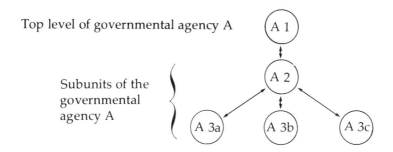

Part B: Multiple Agencies (A,B) and Nongovernmental Actors (X)

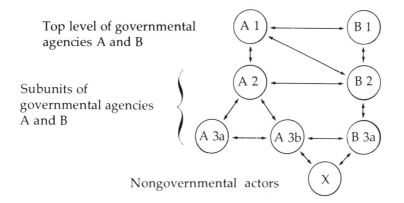

Investigations of the "what's happening?" type assume there are a rich variety of factors that can and do
influence implementation. These studies want to discover
and specify these factors. They do not typically begin with a
model of "proper" implementation; rather, they begin (or
end, or both) with a model of influences impinging on
implementation. (For studies of this character see, for example, Pressman and Wildavsky, 1979; Derthick, 1972; and
Ripley and Franklin, 1982).

Generic Questions about Implementation

In many ways a statute should be interpreted as incor-
porating a theory (see Pressman and Wildavsky, 1979:xxi).
Statutes typically say (or at least imply strongly) that if we
do certain things (X), then certain desirable results (Y) will

Figure 5.2

Relationships of Primary Interest in "What's Happening?" Implementation Studies

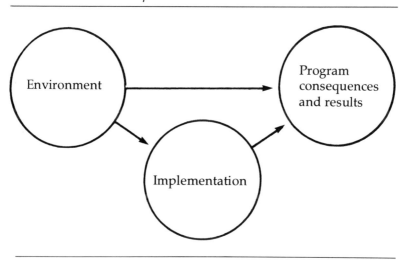

occur. The X in this simple formulation includes specific programmatic treatments and either implies or specifies bureaucratic organizations and processes that will presumably facilitate desirable implementation and target populations who are to receive the benefits. The Y in this formulation includes desired results, which are often left in the form of vague goal statements.

Let's follow through two examples of statutes to give a general flavor of how to think about statutes in this way. In this simple formulation, a job training law might look roughly as follows:

X

Programmatic treatments—job training opportunities through classroom training in specific skills or on-the-job training with specific firms.

Bureaucratic organizations—Employment and Training Administration of the U.S. Department of Labor, state job training organizations, local job training organizations, and a variety of public and private local service delivery agencies.

Processes—such things as mandated private industry councils with certain powers and whose membership meet specified criteria, requirements that program contracts be let only on the basis of competitive bidding, and that governors have veto power over determining local units of government that can take responsibility for programs.

Target populations—disadvantaged people (measured by poverty level income) for most programs and dislocated workers (recently unemployed by plant closings) regardless of previous work history or level of income for programs taking no more than 10 percent of the money.

Y

Desired results—reduce unemployment and shrink welfare rolls.

A similar kind of example in the area of health care makes the same general point.

X

Programmatic treatments—reimbursements of doctors and hospitals for certain kinds of health care for the elderly.

Bureaucratic organizations—federal Social Security Administration and regular medical providers.

Processes—monitoring of fee schedules with federal approval power and selection of health care providers (hospitals, doctors, nurses, insurance companies) by advisory councils.

Target populations—all people over a certain age regardless of income or wealth.

Y

Desired results—improved access for older citizens to needed health care and better health for elderly citizens.

If the above general form of how to think of a statute and its ramifications represents a sensible way to begin thinking about implementation, then a number of general questions can be specified in abstract form that are appropriate for a political scientist who is analyzing implementation to ask and attempt to answer.

A number of questions can be asked that do not necessarily involve field work to collect empirical information (although answers to some of these questions might profit from such field work). Ideally, these questions would be posed before a program actually began so that the answers could be used to improve the chances of successful implementation. In reality, analysts rarely get to ask these questions systematically in timely fashion. These "pre-implementation" questions are not easy to answer because they involve a good deal of judgment about program design. But the judgments made can and should be empirically grounded. These questions include at least the following:

1. Are the components of X defined with sufficient clarity to be understood by implementers?
2. Are the components of X defined in line with reasonable expectations about what might be feasible?
3. Are the components of Y defined with sufficient clarity to be understood by implementers?
4. Is Y, if made more specific, still desirable?
5. Is Y defined in line with reasonable expectations about what might be feasible?

Once implementation has begun, finding out what is happening requires substantial systematic field work. On the basis of this field work data that can help the analyst reach conclusions on the basic questions about implementation and impact can be collected and analyzed. These questions place implementation in its facilitative role, and do not treat it as a phenomenon devoid of any relation to questions of at least short-range program performance and impact (and, possibly, long-range impact).

The central questions to be addressed by the analyst, put in their most simple form, are as follows:

1. Does X lead to Y?
2. Why or why not? (Here is where implementation variables are examined.)
3. To what does X lead instead of or in addition to Y or part of Y?

Political Science and the Evaluation of Implementation

The word *evaluation* when used by social scientists or even by government officials almost always connotes the "evaluation of impact." The position taken here is that social scientists, including political scientists, can be involved fruitfully in the evaluation of many phenomena. Thus, this discussion of political science and the evaluation of implementation begins with a brief discussion of the types of evaluation that can be undertaken. In that context the place of the evaluation of implementation as one of a series of potentially feasible and useful tasks can be assessed.

This general introduction is followed by some specifics on aspects of political science evaluations of implementation, which include a consideration of the types of evaluation and where the evaluation of implementation fits among those types; a discussion of the purposes of the evaluation of implementation; and a consideration of how to conduct field work so as to minimize the chances of getting a distorted view of what is happening and increasing the chances of obtaining a more accurate view.

Types of Evaluation. Evaluation is, for me, a very broad concept because a great deal in the process and content of public policy is subjected to evaluation. The evaluation that gets done, however, may not be formal, and it may not be conducted by social scientists. Much evaluation occurs all the time on the basis of very different kinds of evidence (including unadorned personal preferences) and is done by a variety of people who are involved in making decisions about policies and programs. Social scientists can also engage in evaluation of a broad range of procedural and substantive questions.

Evaluation of processes can take place at any stage. Evaluation of the substantive goals and contents of a policy or program can occur. Evaluation of implementation is potentially valuable. And, of course, evaluation of impact is desirable.

A variety of specific questions of an evaluative character can be addressed by social science analysts, including political scientists. These include the following (although the list is not intended as exhaustive):

- What groups and interests had access in the decisions to establish a policy and program?
- Is the program designed reasonably and well?
- Are the resources provided for the program adequate to give it a chance to achieve its purposes?
- Are preexisting standards for implementation being observed in practice?
- Do intended beneficiaries seek and receive the goods and services designed for them in the program?
- Is the program being administered in accordance with the traditional standards of efficiency and economy? Is money being spent well, honestly, and appropriately?
- Are the processes used in making decisions about the details of the program fair, open, and procedurally correct?
- To what degree has the program achieved its intended goals in terms of impact on beneficiaries?
- Has the program had impacts other than the intended ones on beneficiaries?
- What impacts, both intended and unintended, has the program had on society more broadly defined than just the beneficiary groups?

Where does the evaluation of implementation fit in terms of the rich array of questions deserving evaluation?

One conception—by economist Michael Borus (1979:2)—of social program evaluation will help to focus the discussion. Borus says: "The evaluation of social programs can be divided into three general types, each of which asks different questions but can be thought of as a continuum of steps to trace out the programs' effects. (1) *Process evaluation* asks the question, 'How did the program operate?' (2) *Impact evaluation* asks the question, 'What did the program do?' (3) *Strategic analysis* seeks to answer the question, 'How effective was this program in solving the social problem as compared with all of the other programs directed at the problem?' " Borus also

indicates that the more familiar term "formative evaluation" is similar to process evaluation, and "summative
evaluation" is basically impact evaluation.

The perspective taken here is that the evaluation of
implementation is something partially different from what
is implied by these brief descriptions. Borus stresses the
compliance focus of "process evaluation": "Process evaluation compares the manner in which a program is operated
and the products it produces against the plan for the program. . . . it tests whether the plan is being carried out as
written, on the basis that the plan must be followed in
order to have success."

The compliance focus seems limited. Evaluation of implementation is partially interested in "How did the program operate?"—or, to put it differently, "What happened?" And it is interested in many more aspects of what
happened than just a measurement of what happened
against what was supposed to happen on the basis of law,
regulations, and bureaucratic directives. It is also interested
in at least the short-range aspects of "What did the program do?" Thus, using Borus's terms, evaluation of implementation (1) encompasses process evaluation, (2) asks
additional questions about what happened well beyond a
compliance perspective, and (3) addresses the short-run
aspects of impact evaluation.

The essence of a useful evaluation of implementation
can be stated briefly. It contains:

1. A description of what inputs pass through what processes and result in what outputs (short-run results).
2. An explanation of the patterns of interrelated variables
   observed, in a form as causal as possible.
3. Prescription, if the explanation task has been done
   well. Prescriptive statements necessarily need to focus
   on identifying what policy makers can manipulate and
   what they cannot manipulate, even though they may
   need to understand thoroughly such factors and the
   constraints they place on policy makers.

Not every good study of implementation needs to be prescriptive. However, many should be. Some aspects of implementation are subject to considerable control by implementers. (Although it is often just as important to convince those implementers that they do not have control over all of implementation itself and that they certainly do not have influence, let alone control, over many important contextual variables that may help determine the shape of implementation and impacts, both short-run and long-run.)

Two general contributions can be made by prescriptions stemming from evaluations of implementation. These go beyond the narrower contributions about how to tinker with the implementation processes a bit to achieve more of the desired results and/or dampen some unintended consequence. First, implementation evaluation can help assess the capability of organizations, networks, or organizations and individuals to achieve some things (see, for example, Jones, 1979). Second, in most real decison-making situations in the United States, impact evaluation plays a small role because decisions are usually made before anything like a long-run impact study can be completed (and that, of course, assumes that such a study was commissioned in the first place). This means that if an implementation study, which should include attention to short-run impacts as a dependent variable, is completed, at least some systematic attention to a limited form of impact is available for policy makers to use in debate and decision making.

The mere existence of a study, of course, does not guarantee its use. However, nonexistence of a study paying attention to any form of impact certainly guarantees nonuse! In short, the rough measures of impact, even in the short-run, at least provide some evidence for legislators, bureaucrats, and other policy makers to use in reaching decisions. The danger in using short-run impact measures is, of course, that long-run impact may turn out to move in significantly different directions. This is particularly the case if no theoretical or, especially, empirical work exists that specifies the links between the direction and magnitude of short-run impacts with the direction and magnitude of long-run impacts.

The Purposes of the Evaluation of Implementation. The general purpose of conducting evaluation of implementation by political scientists is to enhance knowledge about the political processes surrounding implementation. There can also be a simultaneous payoff for the managers of the programs being studied in the form of timely and useful information and analysis that otherwise would not be available. Good implementation evaluation helps managers answer the questions (1) what's happening in their programs and (2) what might be done to alter the patterns that appear. Implementation researchers should seek to discern patterns and causal relationships within those patterns, with a particular focus on factors that managers might manipulate in order to change results. Implementation analysis can help guide more pointed and effective managerial interventions.

Implementation research with an evaluative component can serve many specific purposes. These purposes can be summarized as follows:

1. To describe emerging reality in terms of patterns wherever possible.
2. To explain the patterns (influences, direction of influences, and causality, where possible).
3. To evaluate aspects of the implementation process and the early phases of program impact in terms of how well the program has achieved or is achieving a variety of goals, how it stacks up against a variety of expectations, and why it measures up against goals and expectations the way it does. It is important to note that the goals and expectations may come from a variety of sources:
   a. The principal program designers in Congress, the executive branch, and influential interest groups.
   b. Other national actors that may not have helped design the program but are interested in it and may

have influence in future decisions about it. These
actors include, for example, interest groups and national commissions.

c. Critical local actors involved in implementation or
part of or representative of the target beneficiary
groups. These include professional staffs, political
officials, advisory councils, interest groups, and service delivery organizations.

4. To identify and provide advice and recommendations
on policy questions that clearly will recur.

5. To identify and provide advice and recommendations
on broad management questions that are likely to recur
and are important enough to have an actual or potential impact on the content of the policy.

Empirical conclusions, advice, and recommendations
are all tentative in the case of research and evaluation of an
ongoing program. The fact that it is ongoing leaves open
the possibility that the world being studied and evaluated
might change. As long as both the researchers and the
managers looking at the results realize that there is a tentative quality to what is done there is no problem. Managers,
in fact, have the advantage of being able to treat some
changes in an ongoing program as experimental interventions. Research can be specifically directed to picking up the
nature of the impact of such interventions. Thus, some
mid-course corrections in implementation can actually be
tried and evaluated systematically. Evaluations of implementation, impact, or any other policy stage that is completed, by definition, cannot provide such a possibility.

Conditions for the Most Productive Research. Nothing can guarantee that evaluation of implementation research will be of
high quality or that it will be used. (The worst outcome is
for the research to be of low quality and used anyway.)
Several conditions are helpful both in promoting good research and in promoting utilization by managers.

Five attributes of field-based implementation research are particularly desirable. First, as many different instances of the program need to be studied as possible. This gives comparative perspective and means that the oddities, or idiosyncracies, of any one instance of the program will not be transformed into a general view. Having multiple instances of "sites" for study does not eliminate the chance of wrong-headed conclusions, but it at least increases the chances of uncovering general patterns.

Second, it is preferable to have more than one person doing the field work in any given location. This is for the obvious reason that, in this kind of work, two heads (on two different bodies) are likely to be better than one. Any observer in this kind of research can reach mistaken conclusions. There is, therefore, considerable utility in having two or more individuals at a single site collecting data, observing the same phenomena, and hearing some of the same meetings and interviews. If they reach similar judgments, confidence in the accuracy of their conclusions is increased. If they reach differing judgments, they can go back over the data and reassess them to see if there are clues about which interpretation is more nearly correct.

Third, individuals to be interviewed in connection with the implementation of a program at the "street level" (wherever that street may be) should come from different institutional settings and perspectives. Certainly, field research on program implementation that focuses only on interviewing the bureaucratic staff responsible for implementation will run a high risk of getting a distorted view. A wide range of respondents with multiple points of view should be identified and interviewed. Clashing perspectives, values, interests, beliefs, and organizational positions on the part of the interviewees need to be sought. If persons from diverse backgrounds see roughly the same thing, the analyst is relatively safe in concluding what is going on. If there are disagreements, the analyst can either look for the preponderance of evidence (not just from interviewers, but supplemented by documentary evidence, too) or he or she can at least report on different views generated from different sets of interests.

Fourth, interviews are necessarily open-ended much of the time. Open-ended, however, is not equivalent to non-directed or unfocused. Interviewers can and should go to the field armed with specific guides to the areas they want to probe with different categories of interviewees. These guides will specify areas for systematic attention that are deduced both from what is already known and, most important, from expected relationships (hypotheses). Necessarily, field work on implementation is empirical, but it is not uninformed or undirected empiricism.

Fifth, in large-scale implementation evaluations, a group of evaluators will necessarily be involved simply because of the number of sites to be visited and, if funding is available, because each site will require more than one person. These individual evaluators should be treated as a group of colleagues that interact regularly on a variety of topics. All of the evaluators/researchers should discuss such items as: what they are seeing; how to interpret the phenomena they observe; design of the project as a whole (including hypotheses, variables, operational indicators for variables); and design of field work "instruments" such as interview guides, other data collection guides, and debriefing forms for staff members. When reports are written, staff who have been involved in field work should also have responsibility for writing some analytical sections based on field work from all sites, not just their own. The research group, if treated this way, participates fully in the design and execution of a project. Each researcher learns more about research, and the overall research product is likely to be better than it would have been otherwise.

Different models for conducting research incorporate the above features. (For details on one such set of projects, see Ripley and associates, 1977, 1978, 1979 and, for a summary of the findings of eight years of projects conducted along the above lines, see Franklin and Ripley, 1984. For a series of comments on these and other issues, which include some partially different models, see Williams et al., 1982.)

In addition to the above attributes of the research itself, there are two more institutional conditions that help facilitate good implementation research. First, the best work is undertaken by research staffs that have both experience as individuals and continuity as staffs. Simply pulling together an ad hoc group of researchers to undertake a specific field work project is much less desirable than turning to an experienced group of analysts who are already used to working together. In such a staff, turnover can be gradual. Continuing institutional competence should be sought in this area of research. It is desirable in virtually any area. Since implementation is a relatively new area of research, it is worth making the point that the characteristics that help make other research enterprises maximally productive also apply in this case.

Second, this kind of field research is enhanced by the construction and maintenance of ongoing two-way relationships based on trust and confidentiality between those doing the research and those involved in the program, whether as managers or in some other capacity (including those with minority or dissenting views). It is, of course, difficult for a researcher to maintain candid and open relationships with individuals who disagree, sometimes rather bitterly, among themselves. And there is always the danger that the researcher might be coopted by any particularly persuasive point of view coming from a particularly persuasive individual. Having several staff members involved at any given program location is a safeguard in these situations.

Such a close relationship is desirable for two reasons. It can open access to information for the researcher, and it enhances the chances for those who are part of the program to take advantage of potentially useful findings and observations even during a formative stage of the research and some middle stage of the program. Mid-course corrections may, of course, "pollute" the research. But it is foolish to think that social phenomena remain constant for the benefit of the researcher anyway. Any social research project must be sensitive to and account for change no matter what its source. Change that stems from the research itself is no different in character or principle from any other kind of change. I will return to this theme of relationships between the researchers and those being studied in the last chapter of this book when I focus on the "clinical relationship."

Patterns of Interaction and Influence in Implementation

Figures 5.3 through 5.6 portray patterns of interaction and influence in a typical implementation situation in the four domestic policy areas defined in chapter 3. Like figures 4.5 through 4.10, these diagrams portray the actors, the strength of the relationships between them, and the direction of influence in most cases. In one sense these diagrams are rough road maps that allow an analyst to know where to begin to look for politically relevant and important relationships. The maps may be somewhat inaccurate for any specific case, but cover virtually all cases and are never grossly inaccurate. Or, at least, that is the assertion implicit in the presentation of them in this chapter. Like all matters, of course, this assertion is subject to testing on the basis of evidence. If some alternate set of road maps (hypotheses) fits more data better, then these maps should be discarded and replaced by the more accurate ones.

A Few Recent Cases Illustrated

At the end of chapter 4, three cases of domestic policy were outlined briefly to give the reader a feel of the complexity of agenda setting, formulation, and legitimation. In the fol-

Figure 5.3

Patterns of Influence in Implementation of Distributive Policies

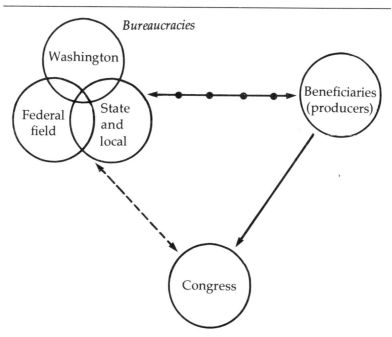

Source: Randall B. Ripley and Grace A. Franklin, *Bureaucracy and Policy Implementation* © Dorsey Press, 1982, p. 196.

Figure 5.4

Patterns of Influence in Implementation of Competitive Regulatory Policies

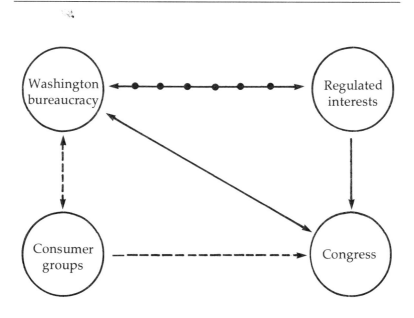

Key:

●—●—● = constantly present relationship; high degree of influence in direction indicated

——— = constantly present relationship; moderate to low degree of influence in direction indicated

– – – = sporadically present relationship; variable degree of influence in direction indicated

Source: Randall B. Ripley and Grace A. Franklin, *Bureaucracy and Policy Implementation* © Dorsey Press, 1982, p. 196.

Figure 5.5

Patterns of Influence in Implementation of Protective Regulatory Policies

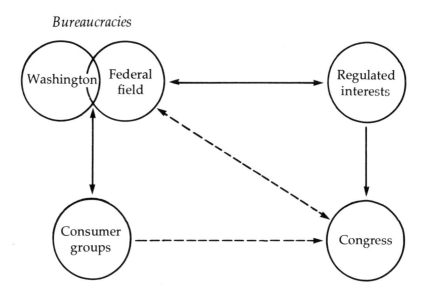

Bureaucracies

Key:

•—• = constantly present relationship; high degree of influence in direction indicated

——— = constantly present relationship; moderate to low degree of influence in direction indicated

- - - - = sporadically present relationship; variable degree of influence in direction indicated

Source: Randall B. Ripley and Grace A. Franklin, *Bureaucracy and Policy Implementation* © Dorsey Press, 1982, p. 197.

Figure 5.6

Patterns of Influence in Implementation of Redistributive Policies

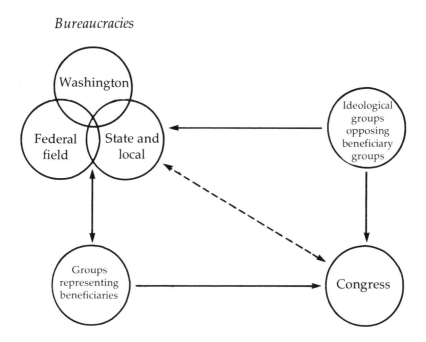

Bureaucracies

Key:

● = constantly present relationship; high degree of influence in direction indicated

___ = constantly present relationship; moderate to low degree of influence in direction indicated

- - - = sporadically present relationship; variable degree of influence in direction indicated

Source: Randall B. Ripley and Grace A. Franklin, *Bureaucracy and Policy Implementation* © Dorsey Press, 1982, p. 199.

lowing sections the implementation stage of these same three policies is summarized briefly, again to give a feel for the complexity of some aspects an analyst must consider.

Water Resources

Implementation of water projects is notable for the high level of participation of congressional subcommittee members in implementation details. Water legislation embodies separate stages in which Congress inserts itself into decisions that are normally in the jurisdiction of implementing agencies. Project proposals originate at the local level, where a large cluster of affected interests mobilizes and articulates support, and then move to the agency and to Congress, where a bill requesting a feasibility study is passed (or rejected). Results of completed feasibility studies (which the agency conducts) are reviewed by the subcommittee, and those deemed feasible are proposed for authorization in an omnibus bill. Determination of the level of funding for projects that have been authorized is a third, but more typical, occasion for congressional involvement.

The high level of congressional participation is paralleled by a low level of executive (presidential or Office of Management and Budget) involvement. Traditionally, the executive has pressed for a greater role in tightening selection criteria in order to reduce costs and unnecessary projects. Congress and the agencies band together to resist such incursions. Both have a stake in keeping the level of funding high and the number of projects large.

The "who benefits?" question is characterized by stability in the generic nature of the beneficiary (local) and by diversity in the specific types of supporters. The diversification of purposes served by water projects generates support from a wide range of beneficiaries—recreation users, electric power users, conservationists, farmers small and large, and navigation and transportation users. The generic beneficiary of water projects has always been "local interests." It is characteristic of pork barrel public works projects that local concerns dominate. The composition of local interests supporting any given project will vary from project to project, but congressional and agency intent is to satisfy a wide variety of local constituencies over time.

Sometimes the interests of multiple constituencies clash, however, and winners and losers emerge. A vivid example is the pressure on the Bureau of Reclamation concerning acreage limitations. In practice, since 1902 the Bureau had exempted large landholders from the 160 acre limit. When pressure in the last two decades built up from conservationists and small farmers to enforce the limit, the bureau under Secretary of the Interior Cecil Andrus temporarily complied in the late 1970s. But counterpressures from powerful agricultural lobbyists reversed the policy at the implementation stage. Congress succumbed, relatively easily, to the pressures of the agribusinesses to increase acreage allotments when the law was amended in 1982.

Strip-Mining Regulation

Implementation of the 1977 strip-mining law has been marked by two distinct contexts or political environments. The first, under the Carter administration, was one in which the support of the administration or enforcement of the law was unquestioned, despite public clamor (led by coal companies) that the nation's energy needs outweighed environmental considerations. The Carter administration was firm in the face of opposition from private industry and even deliberately consorted with environmental lobbyists to defeat a Senate attempt to amend the law in 1979.

The implementation context changed dramatically in early 1981 when the Reagan administration took office. Reagan named a prodevelopment secretary of the interior—James Watt—whose announced goals were to maximize development of energy resources on public lands and to minimize federal regulation in all aspects of Department of the Interior programs, especially those of the Office of Surface Mining (OSM), the agency with implementation responsibility for the strip-mining law.

During the Carter regime, hostile coal companies and states filed multiple lawsuits to contest the validity of the act and of the regulations written by OSM to implement the law. The regulations were extensive, specific, and tough. After two and a half years, only a handful of states had been able to win OSM approval for their surface mining and reclamation plans. Some of the lower court rulings went against the administration, and others were supportive, so the regulated interests had great incentive to keep the situation turbulent and inconclusive by filing more suits. Finally, in June 1981, the Supreme Court ruled in two major cases that the tough regulations written during Carter's tenure were constitutional. Also, during the Carter administration, the House turned back three separate attempts to amend the act. Representative Udall's Interior Committee, which had been instrumental in securing passage of the original legislation, was a vigilant watchdog and prevented attempts to weaken the law. No such watchdog lived in the Senate, and in both 1978 and 1980, a bill to allow states to ignore the regulations was passed in that chamber.

Under the Reagan administration, the political environment was shaped by Reagan's version of federalism: limited federal government involvement (both fiscal and regulatory) and a transfer of program control to the states. These principles were nowhere more honored than in the Interior Department. Watt realized that he lacked the votes in the House to amend the law legislatively, so he exercised a variety of administrative actions that did not require congressional approval to carry out his aim of deflecting the original intent of the law and hobbling implementation. He appointed staff to OSM who were sympathetic to development, not to environmentalist interests. He cut staff levels in OSM, especially in the enforcement unit. He reduced the

OSM budget requests (but Congress gave him more each year anyway—again the House was much more generous than the Senate). Finally, Watt rewrote and diluted all of the regulations governing the implementation of the act. Throughout his tenure as secretary, the level of enforcement was limited. In 1982, a federal district court judge reprimanded him for failure to uphold the enforcement provisions (coal companies weren't the only ones filing lawsuits—environmentalists did too) of the act. The judge ordered the department to collect over $44 million in penalties against seventeen hundred derelict mine operators. But nine months later, only a tiny fraction of the cease-operation orders had been enforced and only $89,000 had been collected. Representative Udall's committee again instructed the secretary to clean up the backlog following oversight hearings.

Employment and Training

Like most legislative compromises, CETA embodied multiple intentions (goals) that were not clearly stated and were not compatible with one another. The principal intentions were to decentralize program planning and administration, to decategorize programs, to target services on the economically disadvantaged, to enhance employability through skills training, and to make local manpower programs more comprehensive. There was slippage in attaining all of these goals/intentions.

Planning and administration were decentralized to local governments, but local administrators' latitude and flexibility were limited even at the outset and shrank over time as the federal government reasserted itself in the administrative realm. Decategorization of programs was likewise weak at the outset, and by 1978 a new set of categorical programs had been created. Service to the most disadvantaged was lower in CETA programs than it had been in MDTA and EOA programs. Training programs' importance was overshadowed by a huge emphasis on public service employment between 1974 and 1979. CETA programs were comprehensive only in name. Major segments of employment and training programs were excluded from the CETA umbrella (Employment Service programs and vocational education programs provide the largest examples).

The interests of clients and potential clients who were the most seriously economically disadvantaged were at least represented during implementation of CETA. Local governments were pressured to curb costs and maximize numbers of people served. The pool of eligible persons was enormous, and local discretion in selecting participants was great. The natural tendency was to enroll the people easiest to train and place. Service to the most disadvantaged was always higher in the basic training title than in the public employment titles, but was lower than the pre-CETA levels of service. Other losers in CETA implementation were manpower advisory planning councils and community action agencies who were service deliverers.

"Winners" in implementation were local governments (prime sponsors) who retained decision-making responsibility until JTPA and whose agencies flourished with employees from public service jobs between 1974 and 1978. The federal government's role was strong initially and grew stronger until JTPA, when it almost ceased. The influence of the private sector began to grow in 1977 and catapulted to prominence in JTPA.

Summary

1. Implementation and impact are more subject to evaluation than are other aspects of the policy process. Yet most of the studies done focus on specific programs. Thus, generalizations about conditions under which different

kinds of implementation and impact are likely to occur are relatively scarce.

2. Implementation studies by political scientists usually focus either on "compliance" of subordinate bureaucratic units to the directives of superior units or on the question of "what's happening?" with a broad set of actors and relationships characterizing implementation processes and politics.

3. The questions in a "what's happening?" implementation study are many and diverse. Dealing with these questions can enhance knowledge about political processes surrounding implementation. Such studies can also benefit managers of ongoing programs in the short run.

4. As with formulation and legitimation, there are predictable patterns of relationships between key actors that vary by policy type. The identity and relative influence of different institutional actors in implementation varies systematically depending on what's at stake.

6

The Nature and Evaluation of Impact

Conceptually, the study and evaluation of implementation overlaps in some respects with the study and evaluation of impact. Evaluating short-run impact (which might also be conceived of as program performance) is an integral part of evaluating implementation.

But there are also many aspects of impact that can and should be studied and evaluated separately. The typical image of an impact study is that a program will be completed or at least have run some years so that impact can be studied on the basis of sufficient data. Collection of such data requires a substantial period of elapsed time. That image is all right, although it needs to be realized that impact is a much broader concept than is normally assumed to be the case. The common model is based on what economists think of when they think of impact. Even political scientists usually accept that view of the nature of impact. The first major section of this chapter will explore the meaning of impact.

The second section of this chapter deals with a kind of evaluation that is particularly amenable to efforts by political scientists. This is "formative" evaluation of social programs. I argue that it is a type of evaluation appropriate for political scientists and that it also has much utility for policy actors. Inevitably this kind of formative evaluation mixes implementation phenomena and some short-run impact (performance) phenomena. The argument in these first two major sections of the chapter is that formative evaluations are particularly appropriate for political scientists to undertake themselves and that summative evaluations of impact, by definition, demand the talents and training of a variety of analysts from a variety of disciplines. No single discipline can provide training by itself that will make any individual or set of individuals able to handle summative evaluation by themselves. Of necessity, all such summative evaluations involve interdisciplinary work. Political scientists certainly can contribute to such summative evaluations, perhaps more than is generally realized in many widely accepted notions of what impact means. But, by definition, political scientists can only make partial contributions to the total effort. Problems of convincing and clearcut causal analyses in conducting long-run impact are never easy to solve. Causation is extremely difficult to prove.

The Meaning of Impact

Impact analysis as practiced in the government and for the government of the United States is a mixed enterprise. Government officials have a natural, understandable, and reasonable itch to know what happened in the programs on which they spent public money. However, the definitions of impact are not well developed among public officials, and certainly they are diverse. For some members of Congress, for example, favorable impact of a program consists of a new building being built or jobs palpably being created in their own district or state. For some bureaucrats, a program with a desired impact is one about which a few favorable anecdotes can be collected that are sufficient to keep congressional patrons happy and congressional over-seers placated and quiescent, while, at the same time, drawing no fire from bureaucratic superiors or interest groups. For some research administrators and in-house government agency research staff, impact rests on short-term indicators of favorable outcomes or outcomes that seem to be moving in a favorable direction. For a few in government and a few professional evaluators outside gov-ernment (usually in universities), impact indicates careful measurement of a number of results over a period of years to prove, or at least to estimate, the degree to which the program is resulting in the desired outcomes. The most sophisticated evaluators are even interested in what results of the program occur that were neither predicted nor desired.

Impact Analysis as Conceptualized and Practiced

An "academic" conception of impact starts by asking the perfectly sensible question, "What did the program do?" (Borus, 1979:3). The assumption is usually made, however, often without being articulated, debated, or de-fended, that "measuring whether the program successfully solved the social problem" involves economic measures vir-tually exclusively. Furthermore, most of the economic measures used apply to the benefits going to individuals. The impact on society is usually measured simply by aggre-gating (or estimating the aggregative effect) of the individ-ual level benefits. Such impact evaluation is often assumed to be the principal kind of analysis worth doing or, in some cases, the only kind of analysis worth doing. This assump-tion is typically made not just by those trained in economics but by those trained in other disciplines too, including political science.

For example, the following kinds of impact measure-ments and analyses take place. Some analyses straightfor-wardly use economic measurements that seem quite appro-priate. Others seem to reach for economic measurements.

1. The average wage gain of graduates from job-training programs. These figures can be converted from hourly wage gains into annual wage gains and, with some estimates, into a net addition to the Gross National Product. In this example, as well as many other cases, desirable impact can be inferred only if a comparison group not receiving the treatment is also studied. For example, everyone, regardless of whether they took job training classes or not, may gain roughly the same in wages over a period of a year or two simply because of inflation and/or a general increase in wage rates. The "treatment" (in this case, the job training program) has to be shown to be a reasonable proximate cause of a significant difference between the treatment group (the trainees) and a similar group in the population at large who did not receive the treatment (training).

2. The economic value of days missed from work (in terms of product not produced) because of illness before implementation of a health care program compared to the economic value of days not missed that would otherwise have been missed after implementation. Again, individual estimates are aggregated into societal estimates and, usually, added to or subtracted from the Gross National Product.

3. The economic value of the added years of productive labor in the work force because of added longevity expectations stemming from public health programs.

4. The economic value of controlling air pollution in terms of the economic value of years/days worked by individuals who otherwise would die or be disabled earlier.

5. The economic value of controlling air pollution in terms of maintenance costs that would not be incurred.

I find this conception of impact focused primarily on individual level economic benefits (with aggregation and with a few measures directly relevant to the collectivity) to be too narrow. However, the scientific instincts about measurement and comparison displayed in these efforts are perfectly sound and deserve emulation no matter how impact is conceived.

The scientific aspiration is often abandoned in practice and all kinds of other "studies" and even nonstudies appear under the guise of evaluation. Let us turn briefly to a consideration of some types of "evaluation studies" that float through both the evaluation community and the bureaucratic and legislative communities.

In the last act of *As You Like It,* Shakespeare has Touchstone, the clown, lay out seven ways of disputing an untruth: the retort courteous, the quip modest, the reply churlish, the reproof valiant, the countercheck quarrelsome, the lie circumstantial, and the lie direct. There is some utility in thinking of the different kinds of flawed evaluations that tend to predominate in real life (not just in social science and evaluation handbooks) in something of a parallel series. Many—not all—of the evaluation efforts can be thought of as one of the following (or some mix):

1. anecdote pure
2. statistic virtuous
3. multiple efforts inconclusive
4. scholar argumentative
5. intuition dominant

A brief consideration of each type of flawed evaluation helps us to see that evaluation is a hard task, both as an intellectual challenge and as a political challenge. There is no pretense in this chapter or anywhere else in this book that good evaluation of impact (or of anything else, for that matter) is easy to achieve.

The Anecdote Pure. A lot of what passes for evaluation that emanates from the government primarily tells stories that are intended to make the program look good. A good example of the anecdote pure type of evaluation appears in a document put out in September 1978 from the Carter White House press office. It was entitled "One Year Later: Carter Administration Youth Employment" and purported to offer an early evaluation of a program that had been passed in August 1977 (the Youth Employment and Demonstration Projects Act). After a few numbers that didn't show much came the short stories of "Danny," "Daphne," and some Job Corps graduates (the Job Corps was a program that had been established for a much longer time and had some successes that could, presumably by inference, shed luster on the whole enterprise of youth work training). A sample: "Daphne, age fifteen, worked in the counseling office at Doherty High in Colorado Springs under the YEDP program. She answered phones, filed and did general clerical work. She is now considering a career in the secretarial field. She tells us that 'there are eight kids in my family so each week I give my Mom some of my pay. I put some in the bank for school next year and if there's any left, I spend it on clothes.' "

Such evaluations presumably make poignant reading, especially by members of Congress or interest groups who are supposed to be impressed. But they say nothing to anyone seriously interested in the impact of a government program.

The Statistic Virtuous. At the other end of a spectrum in terms of data availability and data manipulation are studies that are long and loaded with statistics. These may be ably done, but in the form in which they are presented they may be unintelligible to policy makers and policy actors. This is both because they may be excessively long and because the essence of the evaluative message is not presented in digestible form. To be fair to the researchers, it may also be the case that any attempt to present an "essence" is forced. The findings may be so gray that no message even approaching shades of black and white has much in the way of accuracy to commend it.

I am not arguing that such studies are not worth doing. But it needs to be realized that the chance that they will have much impact in their original form is slim. For recent examples (and there are many), we can turn to the vast outpouring of the multiyear research project sponsored by the Employment and Training Administration of the U.S. Department of Labor called the Continuous Longitudinal Manpower Survey.

Report Number 10 from this project was issued in January 1980. It had about two hundred pages, including the appendices and other matter. It had complex tables in support of the findings and made an appropriately detailed analysis of the findings. The "summary" was fifteen pages long and included three tables, each of which was three and one-half pages long (in very small type). The report itself and the project were good, but the average "line" bureaucrat who saw the report would be likely to conclude that some part of CETA was or was not "working" in broad terms if he or she concluded anything. That same bureaucrat would almost surely abandon that opinion quickly if he or she perceived a different opinion on the part of a key member of the House or Senate. The individual study cited and the other studies emanating from CLMS provided a statistical picture of some aspects of CETA. The effect of this evaluation was minimal. (And, in fact, the report picked as an example of the whole project was virtually completely descriptive of people who enrolled in CETA in 1977–78). "Evaluation" came only around the edges and mostly indirectly.

Another example of elaborate evaluation that would be hard to include in a debate over options was provided by the careful work on the negative income tax experiment in New Jersey and Pennsylvania in the 1970s. The original report was about two thousand pages long in 8½ x 11 inch format. It spawned a series of scholarly books and journal articles. This output was well done but did little to inform debate among officials, let alone a broader public.

The Multiple Efforts Inconclusive. Any individual study can, of course, be inconclusive in what it finds. There are a few areas, however, in which there are multiple studies, and each individual study has some definite, concrete findings. The findings of individual studies may directly contradict each other in some instances. Cumulatively, the bottom line is unknown for one or more reasons.

A good example of this phenomenon is in the field of education. A headline over a detailed article by a sophisticated education writer for the *New York Times* a few years ago (November 13, 1977) captures an accurate assessment: "No One Knows What Makes a Good School." In the article, Fred Hechinger summarizes the findings from a number of different "good" evaluations of the impact of a variety of independent variables on school quality and result of education. These variables included such items as class size, school size, teacher experience, teachers' race, teachers' salaries, per-student expenditure, school facilities, and heterogeneity of student body. The studies agreed on virtually nothing and flatly disagreed on some items. On many items the findings were inconclusive.

Diane Ravitch (1983), in her comprehensive review of developments in American education from 1945 through 1980, has several similar conclusions about social science evaluations in her lengthy "Note on Sources" at the end of the book. In speaking of the many studies of race and education, she says: "Written in the midst of social crisis, these analyses form a specific body of literature, with common assumptions and common terms of reference. Unhappily, there have been few efforts to evaluate this work as a whole, to see whether its assumptions and prescriptions are valid when removed from the context of crisis" (p. 365).

Similarly: "Another angle of vision on the reforms of the late 1960s is provided by federally funded program evaluations. . . . Hundreds, probably very many hundreds, of evaluations have been sponsored by the federal government since the passage of federal aid to education in 1965. Some of these evaluations turn out to be rather wonderful documents for the historian of the future, with plenty of detail about curriculum, methods, teachers, students, the community, and efforts to introduce changes. Unhappily, the evaluations for some federally funded projects . . . are difficult, if not impossible, to obtain" (p. 368).

The Scholar Argumentative. Some evaluators, even if housed in universities, appear to be setting out to structure studies that make specific political arguments. At least they are charged with proceeding in that fashion.

Education again offers good examples of individuals who presumably undertake evaluation but seem more intent on making political statements. For example, Kenneth Clark (1973) attacks Christopher Jencks et al. (1972) in his study of race and education for attempting to achieve "social science validation through public relations" (p. 116). What Clark and Jencks disagree about, fundamentally, is their views of the relation of race to educational questions.

An even more durable example of a social scientist who has remained constantly in the public eye (at least of that part of the public that gets exercised over the relation of education to things like integration, busing, and the tax standing of private school tuition) is sociologist James S. Coleman. In a study in the mid-1960s (1966), he and his colleagues suggested that integrated schools promote better education. In subsequent studies he became the darling of the conservatives, because he first indicated that busing created white flight (1975), which worked against the viability of the public schools, and then he found that students attending private schools got better educations and were better disciplined. He also coupled the production of major studies with an active public speaking career on behalf of the policy recommendations he felt stemmed from his findings.

Close observers of the relationship of such scholarly reports to the political furores to which they "contribute" raise an interesting set of questions about the responsibility of evaluators of sensitive subjects. Fred Hechinger (*New York Times*, May 11, 1981) puts his view this way in commenting on Coleman's work:

"Sociology at its best is the study of the development and structure of society and social relationships. While not a precise science that can predict behavior, it is nonetheless a valuable discipline assisting the search for more rational social arrangements.

"Sociologists invite trouble, however, when they break out of such a useful supporting role into the stardom of advocacy based on their fallible predictions. The fact that they can walk away from a failed policy and go back to the drawing board—a luxury politicians can't afford—underscores the risk of too close a relationship between research and policy making."

Edward Fiske, also writing in the *New York Times* (January 8, 1980), makes the same point in a slightly different form, also in the context of commenting on Professor Coleman's political involvement:

"How responsible are social scientists for the way their findings are used by politicians and other policy makers?

"The question—an old one in nuclear physics and other natural sciences—has been raised by recent studies of the effectiveness of urban schools. It is an increasingly important issue, complicated by the fact that the conclusions of much social science research are ambiguous and even self-contradictory."

The Intuition Dominant. When all is said and done probably the most normal mode of evaluation of impact used by policy actors and officials working in some stage of the policy process relies on intuition and/or political ideology. It has become somewhat unfashionable to state intuitive or political "evaluations" of impact as the reason for decision. Rather it is more fashionable to wrap those intuitions or ideological beliefs in the guise or under the cover of some sort of more formal evaluation. For example, when President Nixon sought to cut back the Job Corps—a Great Society creation of the Johnson years—he relied heavily on a confidential evaluation by Secretary of Labor George Schultz (see Ripley, 1972:82–83). His evaluation was, in turn, buttressed by some findings in a General Accounting Office (GAO) study. But what he was really developing was the political view of the Nixon administration toward this specific program set in the context of a general position toward Great Society domestic programs. Fortunately

for Nixon, the political views and intuitions did not conflict with one applicable and visible evaluation: that by the
GAO.

An even more clear instance of the supremacy of
intuition and ideology when they might conflict with the
contents of evaluation studies came in the first year of the
Reagan administration. During the 1960s and especially in
the 1970s, the Department of Labor had been aggressive in
commissioning many impact studies of the major employment and training programs supported by DOL dollars.
In the 1970s these programs were, for the most part,
clustered around various aspects of the Comprehensive
Employment and Training Act (CETA). Many of those
studies showed that the training programs, despite some
problems, were in general having a desirable impact on
the trainees. They were, in a word, "working." (Evidence
was more mixed on the public service employment parts
of CETA.)

In early 1981 the Reagan administration, in effect, announced that they wanted to end CETA totally and replace it
with no federal effort in employment and training. They
later compromised on what became the Job Training Partnership Act of 1982, but their first preference was for no program (see Baumer and Van Horn, 1984: ch. 6).

In late 1981, a reporter for the *Washington Post* asked
the assistant secretary for employment and training why
the administration persisted in its anti-CETA program
positions when the latest studies showed the program had
overcome most of its problems and was working well. The
assistant secretary's answer is revealing (quoted in the
Washington Post, December 29, 1982): "There are many
CETA reports that are coming in now. . . . We have our
own ideas and, quite frankly, we're not going to play our
hand until we see how things shape up." He juxtaposed
the "ideas" of the administration—which pushed in one
direction—with "reports" that he identified, according to
the reporter, with the previous administrations because
they had commissioned the research. In this conflict, in his

view, "ideas" (or read "ideology" or "political beliefs") were superior to "reports" (read "formal evaluation").

A Broader Conception of Impact

When anyone studies program impact, what kinds of things should he or she look for? When political scientists help in the assessment of impact, what phenomena should they have in mind, in general, and with which phenomena are they most suited to deal?

The commonly accepted meaning of impact (even among scholars from different disciplinary and training backgrounds) involves economic phenomena and, for the most part, measurement at the individual level, with societal impact simply an artifact of aggregating individual level information. It misses many important phenomena and also biases the selection of policy and program goals toward those that can be conceived of and measured in this limited way.

There are at least four major dimensions of impact. The first three are really spectra, although they can be conceived of in nominal categories, too. The four dimensions involve (1) time; (2) relation of actual impact to intended impact; (3) aggregative level of impact; and (4) type of impact. I will discuss each of these dimensions briefly.

Time. The time of impact is important to specify in any specific inquiry. Different expectations are reasonable at different time periods after the initiation of a program. Different measures are also reasonable. Naturally, the longer the post-initiation period being studied, the more difficult it may become to measure impacts (because the chain of causality becomes obscure, and the number of other influences that may explain what is happening increases rapidly). If longer term effects on individuals are studied, there is the practical problem of keeping track of the same individuals over a long period of time. But the intellectual problem cannot be wished away. In fact, everyone should expect a changing range of impacts *over time* from programs.

Politically, of course, long-run impacts simply take a while to work out. The "evaluation" of such impacts that takes place may be wholly political. For example, it is clear that several generations of Americans—virtually everyone by now—made the decision that supporting the older members of their families would be a great burden without the old age and survivors' insurance feature of the Social Security system created in 1935. When presidential candidate Barry Goldwater attacked Social Security in 1964 or presidential candidate Ronald Reagan attacked Social Security prior to his nomination in 1980, a widespread and intense negative reaction to their position became evident in short order. Those who attacked Social Security either quickly recanted or they suffered negative political consequences. Goldwater probably suffered a net loss of votes in 1964 on the issue. Reagan backpedaled quickly and skillfully before the 1980 election and by 1983 could sponsor a commission and subsequent legislation to "bail out" the system and, presumably, make it secure for future generations.

Analysts of impact almost never can study a wide variety of time periods simultaneously. Any individual study must specify what time period(s) is (are) being addressed.

Relation of Actual Impact to Intended Impact. Analysts of impact need to pay attention not only to the degree to which a program achieves what it is intended to achieve but also to effects the program might have that are not intended (or even thought about), that are intended only in part, or that are the opposite of what is intended. It is difficult to ascertain with some degree of certainty the actual effects of a program compared to the intended effects. It becomes even more difficult to deal with effects no one thought about ahead of time or effects that push in an opposite direction. Yet, these are all aspects of impact.

For example, the purpose of the mortgage insurance portions of the National Housing Act (1934) and the mortgage insurance programs of the Veterans Administration after World War II was primarily to increase home ownership among the American population. Analysts can show that the programs had that desired result. Home ownership was increased.

However, only after the fact (many years after the fact) did analysts begin to ask questions about what other effects (presumably not intended) stemmed from these mortgage guarantee programs. When they began to exercise their imaginations, assess social trends, and look at a wide variety of data, they concluded that these programs also helped promote the growth of suburbs, the decay of central cities, and an increased gap between the quality of housing that could be bought or afforded by white Americans compared to that available to minority groups, especially black Americans.

Aggregate Level of Impact. Impact can be studied in relation to individuals, and individual level impacts can be aggregated and averaged and analyzed in various ways to give some sense of what is happening to a larger subset of individuals or, looked at another way, a larger subset of society. But larger groups in society or society as a whole can also be the subject of impact and can be studied directly by analysts, although measurement of such impact presents even more than the normal set of major problems.

For example, it is quite possible to say something about the impact of a welfare program on the target population at the individual level. Something can also be said about the impact on that population and potential welfare population more generally. But something also needs to be said about the impact on society in general. What difference does the size of the welfare population make? Does that size and the manner of welfare affect the attitudes and the political and social behavior of the nonwelfare part of the population?

Type of Impact. There are at least four major types of impact of domestic programs that social scientists can examine: on economic well-being; on decision-making processes; on public attitudes such as support for the political system; and on quality of life. Political scientists are particularly well trained and suited to undertake examinations or play leading roles in undertaking examinations of decision processes and attitudes.

It is certainly appropriate to look for economic impacts of programs both on individuals and on society in general (and on subsets of the general population). Income, value added, cost-benefit ratios, expected earning power, Gross National Product, and similar concepts are all appropriate units of measurement when economic impact is being sought and analyzed.

Policies also have impacts on the processes by which subsequent policy and program decisions are made. Because of the impact of previous policies, processes may become relatively more open or more closed in terms of access by individual citizens, nongovernmental groups, and intended beneficiaries. For example, one concrete impact of the "war on poverty," even though that "war" did not come close to eliminating poverty, was to help mobilize and train groups and individuals who had previously been excluded from any role in policy making and program decisions, even though the programs and policies affected them to a considerable extent. Programs in the 1970s and 1980s dealing with the poorer classes in society were influenced by the change in processes wrought by the access of these newly savvy individuals to some decisions.

Policies and programs affect the attitudes of people in several senses. Both those who are supposed to benefit and the general public have attitudes toward specific programs, toward governmental effectiveness and legitimacy in general, toward specific officials and offices, toward their own sense of well-being, and toward their own ability to achieve what they want in life. Attitudes toward governmentally sponsored programs or generated in part by such programs have importance in the functioning of those specific programs and on the policy and program choices and decisions made by the society and by specific officials in the future. These attitudinal impacts are well worth studying and analyzing.

Finally, policies and programs have important impacts on the general quality of life for individuals, for groups of individuals in society, and for society as a whole. Measurements of these impacts often should be noneconomic. Matters such as availability of leisure time, availability of different kinds of pursuits and opportunities for enriching one's life and spending one's leisure time (for example, libraries, art galleries, musical organizations), literacy, health, and the existence of opportunities for various kinds of education throughout one's life are all examples of the kinds of concerns that must be addressed by an analyst working in this area.

Not every program has every kind of impact affecting all points on all dimensions. Even if programs have all of these impacts in principle, it may be inefficient or just foolish to pursue the analysis of all of them. The analyst must make choices about what is worth analyzing and then set out to measure key concepts and conduct the appropriate analyses. Too often decisions about what to analyze are made unthinkingly on the basis of simply accepting the superiority of economic measures. Or, worse yet, decisions about what to measure are made on the basis of what data are available.

Designing and Conducting Formative Evaluations of Social Programs

One kind of evaluation, which involves some impact evaluation and also other kinds of evaluation, is a formative evaluation of social programs, particularly when the program in question is new or relatively new. Formative evaluations take place in the early stages of a program—literally when it is still forming. Summative evaluations take place at the end of a program or at least when it has matured to the point that its effects can be summarized. Formative evaluations are particularly suited to the mix of skills acquired by a political scientist interested in policy analysis. Such a study can enrich the understanding of political processes and, at the same time, make the social scientists doing the evaluations of direct use to individuals whose job it is to make the programs as effective as possible.

This kind of evaluation is, of course, not the only kind in which a political scientist might be involved, but it is potentially important enough for political scientists to warrant a discussion of such a study. The discussion that follows first describes the general pupeses of formative evaluations. Second, it comments on the sources of goals and expectations. Third, it offers some comments on how to move from study design to operational status. Fourth, it comments briefly on the importance of field work to the ongoing shaping of the project. And, finally, it summarizes the nature of formative evaluations. (For concrete examples of formative evaluations, see Ripley and associates, 1977, 1978, and 1979.)

Purposes of Formative Evaluations

The purposes of evaluative studies in relation to implementation were discussed in chapter 5. The formative evaluation described here is both an evaluation of impact and an evaluation of implementation. The purposes of the study are about the same as those already discussed in chapter 5 and need not be repeated in detail. To recapitulate, however, the major purposes are:

1. To describe emerging reality in terms of patterns wherever possible.
2. To explain the patterns in terms of both influences on and causes for them.
3. To evaluate aspects of the implementation processes and the early phases of program impact in terms of

how well the program is achieving a variety of goals. The concern of the analysts is both for how it stacks up against a variety of goals and expectations and *why* it measures up against various goals and expectations the way it does.

4. To identify broad policy questions and management questions that are important and that will recur (in other words, they are not idiosyncratic) and to offer recommendations based on findings on those recurring questions.

Sources of Goals and Expectations

The importance and relevance of multiple sources for goals and expectations were discussed in chapter 5. That importance and relevance can be underscored here. Formative evaluation is not a test of abstract theories or ideologies, but is related to real world sets of goals and expectations. The analyst, in principle, should not be the captive of any single set of goals and expectations, including those (perhaps particularly those) of the sponsor of the research. A good analyst will seek a variety of goals and expectations from a variety of sources. There almost never is a single universally accepted statement of goals. And all statements tend to be both ambiguous and vague; they also tend to be self-serving in relation to the source making the statement.

Analysts conducting a formative evaluation of a domestic social program in the United States might probe at least the following three major sources of goals and expectations:

1. The principal program designers in Congress, the executive branch, and interest groups.
2. Other national actors not directly involved in program design but with palpable interests in the way in which the program or programs created are implemented (for example, mandated national advisory councils or national commissions).

3.   Non-Washington actors who will have some role to play in implementation, ranging from marginal and supplementary to central. Depending on the nature of the program being studied, these non-Washington actors could be some combination of federal bureaucrats, state bureaucrats, local bureaucrats, state or local executives (for example, governors, mayors, city managers, county commissioners), state and local interest groups, state and local private agencies (both for profit and nonprofit) who contract to deliver program services of some kind, and mandated advisory councils at the regional, state, and local levels.

Finally, if the researcher does not find that the goals and expectations even of a diverse set of groups encompass all of the evaluation questions that seem to be worth asking, then it is quite reasonable for the evaluators themselves—with careful labeling—to insert a few of their own as they design the research.

Moving to Operational Status

Once the evaluators have specified a variety of goals and expectations for the program, from multiple and perhaps conflicting sources, then decisions need to be made about highest priority tasks that should be undertaken and what the evaluators have the competence to do. Not all tasks are desirable, and the evaluators do not necessarily have the competence to undertake even all of the high priority evaluation tasks that are desirable. This may mean that a given evaluation will not be "ideal." In fact, few will. Lost "ideal" components of any study should be dropped by conscious choice, not through inadvertence.

What steps should be taken to move from a series of goals and expectations against which a program might be measured to operational research status? The first step (of seven) is that the researcher should apply several tests of reality as an "ideal" research design is being worked out. The researcher needs to confront the realities of the research situation in developing the research design. "Ideal" research designs are fine as yardsticks in some senses, but it also makes sense to start off in some cases realizing that the ideal designs do not necessarily lead to either the best research or the most useful research (and there is some overlap between the "best" research and the "most useful" research, although those are not identical notions).

A variety of realities should be confronted by the researcher in designing a project and deciding on details of the research design. These realities can be suggested by posing the following questions appropriate to step one.

1. What are the competencies of the staff responsible for research? What are the limitations? Obviously, good research should be designed, and then appropriate research staff should be recruited. However, there is no use ignoring the fact that there are practicalities in what research staffs can be created (depending on who is available, the amount of money for support of the research, and other factors).

2. How long is the study scheduled to run (both in its initial phase and with any projected extensions)? How much of reality and what stages of reality will emerge in time—that is, during the life of the project—to be studied? There is no point including variables and types of impact for study that simply will not be present in measurable amounts (if at all) during the life expectancy of the project.

3. What data limitations of which the researcher is already aware rule out some potential items for study or at least limit what can be done with those items? These data limitations may involve quality, amount, or access. The researcher designing the project should not avoid the most important questions for study because of known data limitations. And, of course, the researchers should use ingenuity in finding surrogate measures where necessary. Ultimately, if some data are simply not available either directly

or in the form of any reasonable surrogate, it makes little sense to include variables relying on that data in the research itself.

4. What did the research director (or principal investigator or project director) and the research sponsor agree to? The typical policy research project is sponsored by an agency or consortium of agencies that have immediate need for and potential use for the results. In developing the grant or contract under which the research is done, the researcher and the sponsor arrive at some agreements on what is to be accomplished. Usually, some "deliverables" (that is, products of the research in terms of reports, handbooks, briefings, and so on) are specified. These are a high priority for the researcher. Add-ons to those deliverables may be acceptable and may be valuable, but it should be remembered that they are add-ons. Major add-ons should be agreed on by sponsor and researcher.

5. What other studies, if any, of the same program are being undertaken? What specific aspects of the program are addressed in other studies? First, redundancy should not be designed into a project unknowingly, but there is often a good purpose served by planned redundancy. For example, it may make sense to have two or more projects examining the most important relationships. On less central matters redundancy may represent a waste of scarce research resources.

As a second step, after taking account of the above limits, the researcher should begin to develop the best possible statement of the variables that are important for the research and how it is hypothesized that the variables relate to each other (a model).

As a third step, once this "limited ideal" is specified, the project designer needs to face concrete operational questions about the variables specified. Once again, a good researcher will balance imaginativeness about data for operationalizing variables with good sense about the limits on the data that can reasonably be expected to be collected.

In step four, the model specified in step two above

should be reviewed in light of what was discovered as the tough, concrete questions about operationalization were faced in step three. It also makes sense to ask the five questions specified in step one again just to make sure there is a considerable element of practicability in the research design that is emerging.

In step five, if the refined model that emerges from step four is too large to work when considered against the practical limits of time and money, the researcher will need to prioritize the research tasks and analyses to make sure the most essential ones get done well.

In step six, once the above five steps are taken, the researcher should be confident that he or she will be able to operationalize the variables in the model and that the model is appropriate as a guide to actual research. At this point the researcher should return to the model to:

1. Pare the "limited deal" model to those variable clusters on which there will be meaningful and appropriate evidence (data).

2. State refined hypotheses linking the variable clusters that remain in the model.

3. Make at least tentative preliminary plans for the specific tests that are intended for application to the hypotheses. If there are no feasible tests for some of the hypotheses, they are probably best discarded. If some of the variable clusters are, therefore, no longer involved in hypothesized relationships with other variable clusters, those clusters can be discarded. Data that lead nowhere in terms of describing and/or testing important relationships have no immediate use and, therefore, no place in an evaluation research project. By the end of this process, the researcher will finally have a working model to guide the evaluation.

Step seven can take place once the working model is in place. Then the researcher can fill in all of the details of required data collection in the field. These details are likely to include design of field work instruments such as interview guides, a list of documents to be gathered, a list of data to be gathered from the files, methods of reporting and analysis, deadlines, and so on.

Additional Questions for Field Work

All of the above procedures allow the research director to specify what the field staff must collect in the field and from documents in order to conduct convincing, meaningful, and pointed evaluative analysis. For other purposes, some other questions may be pursued in the field for one or more good reasons even if those questions are not firmly embedded in the working model. Clearly these additional questions are of lower priority than the information that must be collected.

There are at least three good sets of reasons that some add-on, secondary questions may actually receive some attention in the field research. First, there may be background questions that the field staff needs to pursue for developing its own understanding of the program and decision dynamics being observed. Political scientists (or any evaluators, regardless of discipline) have to know a considerable amount about the context and substance of what they are studying. All programs and all agencies and all actors are not alike. Naturally, political scientists believe in the possibility of generalizing and controlling idiosyncratic features. If they didn't hold such beliefs, systematic program evaluation would be impossible. But such beliefs do not preclude the necessity of being immersed in a subject to prevent egregious, avoidable errors and to provide substantive insight that can be applied to relationships that otherwise would be arid and extremely abstract.

Second, there may be questions about which the research sponsor feels an immediate need to know and that the researchers agree (1) are important, (2) are within the scope of competence of the research staff, and (3) the provision of which will not jeopardize any of the more central elements of the evaluation (for example, access or

Table 6.1

The Nature of Formative Evaluations of New Social Programs

Is Not	Is
1. Purely hypothetico-deductive or purely empiricist.	1. Highly empirical—but guided by statements of expected relationships and relationships thought to be important by both the researchers and "real world" people positing both explicit goals and expectations.
2. Purely an academic exercise.	2. Policy research with disciplinary and policy values for multiple publics.
3. Dogmatic or ideological in origin, design, intent, or execution. However, it is also not "value free."	3. Aimed at addressing numerous questions with normative dimensions *as long as those questions are within reach*—that is, questions on which we can expect to have convincing, empirically grounded statements to make, and the normative dimensions of which we can discuss without taking the view that we know and are prepared to announce and propagate "The Truth."
4. Ignorant of reality through unbending adherence to a fixed research design.	4. Cognizant of reality and able and willing to adapt the research design to that reality.
5. Seeking as an end product a single cosmic judgment of success or failure of the program.	5. Making a series of evaluative/judgmental statements with varying degrees of certainty based on what we know empirically. Some of those statements can (and probably should) be in the form of: if you want to achieve goal A, process X is an inefficient way to do it but process Y is an efficient way to do it.
6. Rigid in design or execution in any sense.	6. Flexible in design and execution in many senses.

good relationships with key informants and actors or meeting other, more important deadlines in the project). There may be some tension in this area between sponsor and outside supported researcher. Bureaucrats tend to look for help with the questions they need answered immediately. These questions may involve only low-level description or program monitoring. Social scientists engaged in research need to refuse, nicely but firmly, to become involved in such tasks. On the other hand, some add-ons requested by sponsors are appropriate in several senses, and there is no reason the research team cannot undertake them.

Third, reality changes. New phenomena (variables) may turn out to be important even though they were not specified ahead of time. An evaluation research project needs to retain the flexibility to identify and to pursue questions related to such variables. If preliminary explorations suggest that the questions are of sufficient importance, they can then be inserted into the general analytical scheme through the modification of the working model and related specifications about data collection and analysis.

The Nature of Formative Evaluations of New Social Programs: A Tabular Summary

The essence of what the kind of research just discussed both is and is not can be summarized in tabular form. Table 6.1 contains that summary.

Summary

1. The study of impact is not as clearly in the expert province of political science as is the study of implementation. But some studies of impact can use political science knowledge profitably.

2. As embedded in real studies, impact tends to be conceived of in purely economic terms.

3. A meaningful rounded conception of impact includes the major dimensions of time, relation of actual impact to intended impact, aggregative levels of impact, and type of impact.

4. The types of policy impacts amenable to examination by social scientists include those on economic well-being, on decision making processes, on public attitudes, and on quality of life. Political scientists can be especially important in examining decision processes and attitudes.

5. Political scientists can be especially effective in evaluating programs that are still in the process of forming. These evaluations can deal with short-range preliminary impacts. The most important theoretical problem to solve in such studies is to link the short-run impacts to predicted long-run impacts in a convincing fashion.

7

The Policy Analytic
Task

This book contains several lines of argument as a way of promoting thinking about policy analysis in political science. It is not a "how to do analysis" book. It is a book that encourages consideration of the problems of how to think about analysis in a discipline and how to think about people trained in that discipline as policy researchers.

In this chapter, I will finish the major lines of argument. The five sections that follow will:

1. Discuss the meaning of the utilization of policy analysis done by social scientists, including political scientists.

2. Summarize the areas of the policy process in which political scientists can be useful.

3. Examine some of the general conditions promoting and constraining access for the analyst.

4. Summarize the nature and extent of sponsorship of social science research, especially policy research, and the broad impact of that sponsorship on the policy analysis component of political science.

5. Outline the nature of the "clinical relationship" between policy analysts and policy makers as providing a framework that is potentially fruitful for both parties.

The Utilization of Analysis and Evaluation

In this section, I will discuss the meaning of utilization, conditions that increase the chances of utilization defined broadly, and the value of pursuing utilization defined in the way I do. Let me begin the discussion simply by noting that there is no widely agreed on definition of research utilization, especially when it applies to the research of social scientists. I begin this discussion assuming the dominant role of nonresearch, political considerations in decision making about public policy in the United States. I do not bewail that fact. But an acceptance of that fact does lead to a modest view of what policy research can achieve in terms of "utilization," even broadly defined. If utilization is conceived of in a narrow sense, an acceptance of the dominance of political considerations leaves almost no room for utilization of research outside of attaching it to the support of specific political judgments.

The Meaning of Utilization

Various people have written persuasively that utilization has several meanings (see, for example, Knott and Wildavsky, 1980; Patton, 1978; Weiss, 1979; and Weiss, 1980; for a fine summary of the literature, see Rosenthal and Van Horn, 1982; for a recent conceptual and empirical exploration, see Wright, 1984). Different parts of policy-relevant research can be "used," including (1) the description and/or analysis itself, (2) the empirical findings, and (3) the recommendations stemming from the research. Any one, a combination of two, or all three elements of policy-relevant research can be used in some way by policy actors.

Obviously, any single study can be used. It is also true that a series of studies or portions of a series of studies—either by the same or by different researchers—can be used.

Parallel series of studies coming out at roughly the same time or even at different times can also be used.

If the above simple points are accurate, then clearly the notion of "measuring" utilization by simply using the model of the impact of discrete research study X on discrete policy or program decision Y makes no sense. It also makes no sense on the basis of what we know about how policy makers and implementers react to policy analysis.

Furthermore, I would argue that the notion of utilization of study X on decision Y in a linear way makes no sense intellectually either. Even in the academic world, literature typically builds up cumulatively. Evidence, methods, and findings are assessed as they come from many studies over time. The "piece of knowledge X affects subsequent action or belief Y" model is inappropriate in the diffusion of knowledge in universities and academic disciplines, just as it is in courts of law, in bureaucracies, in legislatures, and with other potential users/consumers of policy research.

A number of scholars (see, for example, Lynn, 1978; Lasswell, 1971; Janowitz, 1972; and Crawford and Biderman, 1969) have written about the "cumulative impact" of policy research, "guiding the focus of attention" of policy actors, and the "enlightenment function" of social science policy research. All of these notions are appropriate. They describe a long-range, cumulative pattern of utilization that serves to enlighten the user about specific relationships and patterns.

In short, it is not reasonable to expect any single piece of policy research to have much impact or immediate concrete impact. This is, in part, because any single piece of research almost surely will have a narrow design, focus, and data base. No single study deserves to be taken as "gospel." Problems can arise in the few exceptional cases in which a single study is taken too seriously. Any information coming from policy research—either one study or a series or collection of studies—is only one input source among many. Even if the work and the analysts doing the work are respected and taken seriously, decision makers inevitably have lots of other sources of information to which they pay attention: instincts; anecdotal evidence; personal preferences; the preferences of superiors, subordinates, and equals in a formal sense; and the preferences of a whole host of actors involved in any given decision or set of decisions.

In a sense, then, it may be misleading and probably foolish to try to look for the definable and measurable impact of a single piece of policy research on a specific decision. Someone interested in identifying utilization should look for patterns of utilization over time. There is a practical problem here: many agencies that, logically, should be users of policy research do not sponsor some sort of program of research, analysis, and evaluation—that is, an interconnected series of projects that describe and analyze the policy world the agency inhabits. Rather, they sponsor only discrete individual policy projects. And, of course, some agencies do not even go that far. They sponsor nothing. As indicated above, discrete studies have a slender chance of being utilized within a sponsoring agency let alone by anyone else. Only the results of a research program that contains individual studies as its component parts have much chance (although far from a certainty) of affecting the way policy makers and program implementers think and behave. The Department of Labor (DOL) had a research program in the 1960s and 1970s. The programs of DOL, especially those of the Employment and Training Administration (ETA), were affected (on this program and some of its impacts through utilization, see Hargrove, 1980, and Committee on Department of Labor Research and Development, 1975).

In the 1980s, the DOL pattern of sponsored research shifted dramatically to one of supporting a few discrete studies. The short-run impact of research on program decisions in DOL quickly diminished. Utilization in the sense of enlightenment will also wither over time. In many ways, of course, members of the Reagan-appointed layer of DOL are suspicious of social science research because they view the researchers and the products of their work as innately favorable to Democratic (and thus, unacceptable) alternatives.

A "program of research" is, of course, costly compared to sponsoring only a few discrete studies. On the other hand, the amount of money spent on any kind of social science research is trivial compared to program money (for example, at a time when the whole research effort of DOL, primarily ETA, was costing about $150 million [FY 1980] CETA alone was spending between $8 and $10 billion annually).

So far I have talked about and around the concept of utilization. Now it is appropriate to come down with as fixed a definition of research utilization as I think describes the phenomenon in a sensible, but inevitably somewhat vague way. Utilization of policy-relevant research means that some policy makers and policy actors:

1. Read or at least are aware of some parts of some policy-relevant research and analyses.

2. Think about the meaning of some of the parts of these analyses in making concrete decisions *or* in appreciating the options that seem to be open to them *or* in defining the options that are open to them.

Utilization looks a lot like enlightenment to me. Defined in this way it is, of course, extremely difficult to measure, but concepts should come prior to measurement problems.

Conditions That Increase the Chances of Utilization

At least four major sets of conditions increase the chances of utilization as broadly defined in the preceding section. First, the chances of utilization increase when the ruling paradigms of an agency and/or the program being studied are not challenged. Agency bureaucrats usually hold two assumptions, often unexpressed and almost always unexplored. One of these assumptions is that the existence and the mission of the agency are valuable and virtuous. The other is that the program for which they are responsible and that is being studied can be made to "work" if the bureaucracy will only function correctly. They further assume that the program will do some good when in "working" order.

Studies that do not challenge either of these basic assumptions may be taken seriously even if they are critical of some aspects of what is happening or not happening. But studies that raise questions about the utility of the agency or parts of the agency and about the wisdom and utility of the design of a program under review are ignored. The evaluators are often branded as "cranks" or simply regarded as ignorant of some of the important verities of life.

If I may be autobiographical for a few paragraphs it is worth contrasting the different reactions of the Department of Labor to a series of policy analyses I directed between 1974 and 1981 with DOL financial support. Most of the studies were of pieces of CETA and challenged (for good reason, I would argue) neither of the basic assumptions above. However, one study my group completed did challenge the second assumption. This was a study of the Targeted Jobs Credit Tax program (see Ripley and Smith, 1979). Our central finding was that the program was so badly designed that no matter how much effort was put into it by individuals at the federal and especially at the state and local levels, which were responsible for implementation, it simply could not achieve very much. Localities that tried hard and localities that did not try at all would do about equally well in terms of having any impact. Variations between performance in localities were random. This finding flew directly in the face of the belief/assumption of the federal bureaucrats that any program could work and that their own performance was the key to how well it worked. Of course, the finding also flew in the face of the political reality that there were a few interest groups and a few well-placed members of Congress eager to extend and expand the program. Thus, our efforts were met with a mix of indifference, non-understanding, and hostility. We had clearly passed over an allowable boundary in our policy analysis.

A second atypical experience in the eight years we worked on employment and training problems with Department of Labor support occurred in terms of the reaction of those who made decisions about how to spend research dollars (a mix of "line bureaucrats" and "research bureaucrats") to several proposals from us to study the workings of the regional office structure of the Employment and Training Administration. By the time we made those proposals we had done a lot of policy work with ETA support. By and large, the work was well received and had had some modest utilization as part of the broader ETA research program. But the proposals to study the regional offices were met with disbelief and/or hostility because the unstated assumption was that the study might show that the regional offices (a major part of ETA) had only limited utility. This was viewed as a threat to the agency, even though many of the most senior bureaucrats in Washington had serious doubts about regional performance. They were quite willing to criticize aspects of regional office behavior. They were quite unwilling to face even the possibility of findings that would suggest a major realignment of the agency (and I have no idea that that is what we would have found). Ironically, the Reagan administration drastically cut back all of ETA, including large chunks from the regional office operations. But this was a political challenge that those in the agency could understand and try to combat. An intellectual challenge, or even proposed research that conceivably could result in an intellectual challenge, was outside the pale of acceptable policy research.

A second condition that increases the chances of utilization in a bureaucracy is the lack of involvement or interest of the legislature (Congress, of course, in the federal example). Congress is almost uniformly threatening to high level federal bureaucrats, and bureaucrats assiduously listen for hints of congressional preferences. If they get those hints or even think they hear hints of preferences, they are unlikely to be interested in using the findings stemming from programs of policy research, unless, of course, the findings from that research program reinforce the biases and beliefs perceived to be held by the most important congressional actors.

Third, the chances of utilization increase when the political masters in the bureaucracy or the senior civil servants to whom they delegate various responsibilities have some commitment to using empirically derived knowledge in their decision making. At minimum, they must have at least neutrality toward such knowledge. What almost surely will be fatal to utilization is hostility to such knowledge. Such hostility could be based on a number of things: self-pride in the superior intuition of the self-made person who becomes, for example, an assistant secretary when compared to the "book learning" of university research scholars; an impatience with abstract findings; and ideological conflicts between the political appointees and what they perceive to be the ideology of the research community working in their substantive area.

Fourth, the chances of utilization increase when researchers and the consumers/sponsors of the research are engaged in what I call a clinical relationship. I will return to a fuller description of and comment on that relationship in the last section of this chapter.

The Value of Pursuing Utilization

If the deck is stacked against much visible, immediate, and direct utilization (even utilization conceived of as enlightenment is fragile and requires some special conditions to have much chance), the natural question is whether scholars should bother to make the effort. I think some scholars some of the time can reasonably have three major sets of reasons for pursuing research that should be able to contribute to "enlightenment" utilization for policy actions. First, research aimed at policy questions that contains a component that might be utilized in this broad sense sometimes addresses interesting and important research questions that otherwise would not be addressed on the basis of systematic empirical research. The reason for this net addition to the research agenda is simple: this kind of research takes money, and only agencies are likely to fund it. Otherwise, the research will almost surely go unfunded and, therefore, undone.

Second, researchers have an opportunity through this kind of work to broaden their future research agenda by what they learn from their interactions with their sponsors and, particularly, their interactions with the programs and their interviewees (formulators, implementers, target population, and anyone else involved in a policy or program). Third, there is for some researchers a challenge to the enterprise of trying to add "enlightenment" to the stew of considerations taken into account during all of the various stages of decisions in the policy process. Some, no doubt, hold the view that a bit of systematic evidence absorbed by policy actors over time is better than no such evidence.

Relative Analytic Contributions in Different Policy Stages

In chapter 5, a table (table 5.1) was presented that summarized the relative amount and type of attention to the four major policy stages in two general kinds of policy studies literature—that which is primarily descriptive and analytic in character and that which is explicitly evaluative. Here we want to add a somewhat different twist to an impression of what political scientists can do in relation to the different policy stages. Table 5.1 summarized what the literature already holds. Here our concern is with what level of contributions can reasonably be expected regardless of the performance to date.

In dealing with agenda building, political scientists working within the traditions and confines of questions

generated simply by virtue of appropriate disciplinary interests can do a fair amount. The disciplinary literature on
agenda building to date is thin. Some promising work suggests that a good deal more can be done. On the other
hand, evaluative studies of agenda building are unlikely to
have much impact. The agenda-building processes involve
major social forces and actors. As suggested in chapter 1,
there is not much reason to expect empirical or prescriptive
contributions that will be utilized, even in the broad sense
of that term used in this volume.

In addressing formulation and legitimation, political
scientists have undertaken and will continue to undertake
studies motivated primarily by questions posed by the discipline. More generalizing and more conceptualization is
needed in this area, but there is no reason it cannot be
achieved. In terms of evaluative studies aimed at promoting
utilization, it is harder to imagine a major political science
contribution, except in relation to specific elements of the
process by which policy is made. Even here, the process
choices made in the real world are heavily laden with politics and values; enlightenment/utilization is not likely to be
interesting to policy actors struggling for advantages that
will lead to formulation and legitimation outcomes that
conform as much to their various preferences as possible.
Thus, it seems unlikely that political scientists will undertake many "practical" studies (that is, empirically based
studies that seek also to base recommendations on the
findings and to get into a stream of findings and reports to
be "utilized"). The few that are undertaken are likely to be
ignored.

Another kind of study of formulation and legitimation
results may have more potential. This is the study of the
product of formulation and legitimation—the program as
designed. Scholars do not usually get involved in program
design critiques except inadvertently after doing a study of
implementation or impact or some other aspect of a program. Yet, an early examination of design, based on what is
known about what design features are likely to result in

what kinds of problems and/or successes later on, might have some payoff. Political scientists are probably not likely to play more than a modest role, at best, in conducting such studies. And, as indicated in the previous section, the odds are heavily loaded against policy actors inside the government taking seriously a finding that the design of a program is fatally flawed. Political opponents might take such a finding seriously for their own reasons. But that is a different form of "utilization," one that is more overtly exploitative than most.

In dealing with implementation, there are major possibilities for generating both disciplinary studies and "practical" studies. A fair number of disciplinary studies have already been done, although theory about implementation is in short supply, perhaps because the phenomenon is so extraordinarily complex and the study of it is relatively new. Studies with practical aspects are not yet numerous, in part because most agencies have shown little interest in funding such studies. A few have. But most "practical" aspects of implementation studies represent piggybacking on basic disciplinary studies of the phenomenon. Even if "practical studies" became more numerous, the expected impact would still be modest. In both disciplinary studies and practical studies of implementation, political scientists will be dominant.

Political scientists have been involved only marginally in studies that evaluate program impact. In part this is because impact has been defined almost exclusively in economic terms, and therefore little room has been left for political scientists to make a professional contribution. If the new concept of impact sketched in chapter 6 or at least something like it that goes well beyond economic considerations is recognized as legitimate, there is more room for political scientists to engage in impact studies, both in a disciplinary sense and in a "practical" sense. However, a number of people from a number of different backgrounds in terms of formal training need to study impact. Because of the values in American society it may be that economists always dominate, but political scientists can certainly bring their expertise to bear on some dimensions of impact more broadly defined—especially impacts of programs on future processes and attitudinal impacts of programs. Here too, of course, the expected effect of "practical" studies on "real world" decisions must be accounted as modest.

The Basic Political Situation and Access for Analysts

In chapter 1, I made the point that knowledge and political considerations are closely interwoven. Although academics sometimes pretend that "rational" knowledge and "political" knowledge are totally different, I would argue that they are merely different forms of information, both of which can be brought to bear on policy questions. "Knowledge" is the formally organized result of systematic research and investigation. "Political considerations" stem from personal experience, anecdotal experience, intuitions, payment of political debts through policy and program decisions, creation of supportive coalitions through policy and program decisions, and so on.

Knowledge itself, even when defined in this constricted way, becomes a political variable when it is used in a political process for political purposes. The policy process is inherently political in its major aspects. The image of "objective" or "rational" knowledge struggling with "subjective" political preferences, opinions, beliefs, debts, and judgments is misleading. To be sure, the evidential base for formal policy "knowledge" is different from the evidential base for political considerations, but there is an evidential base for both kinds of information.

None of these comments are intended to deny a tension between those who seek to be more objective, more systematic, and less political (scholars, in most cases) and those who are explicitly political and somewhat wary of the scholars bearing policy recommendations. By the third year of the Reagan administration, for example, there were charges that research grants and awards were being given to politically acceptable researchers rather than to more highly rated scholars without political ties (see, for example, articles in the *New York Times* for September 27, 1983, and October 2, 1983, summarizing the controversy that erupted between the Consortium for Social Science Associations and Reagan administration officials).

At a more abstract level, it seems logical to suggest that analysts are likely to have more access to a policy situation (in terms of the potential influence of their recommendations) if that situation is relatively "quiet." "Quietness" can be defined in terms of low visibility, relatively short duration, low controversy, and the involvement of only a few actors. However, the logical suggestion is probably wrong. A better hypothesis would seem to be that the access of analysts under such conditions is low. If there is little controversy, little chance of controversy because visibility is low, and actors are few, there is no need for analysis. The few people making the decisions agree with each other. Why should they stir up analysis that might point in another direction? Besides, time for decision is short and decisions are made rapidly. Thus, there really isn't much time for analysis either.

If you will recall the discussion in chapter 3 of policy types, this description of "quiet" policy comes close to describing some of the major attributes of domestic distributive policy and structural policy in the foreign and defense arena. It can be hypothesized that one of the forms of knowledge competing for attention in decision making in these two policy arenas is not likely to be that generated by formal systematic analysis. When such analysis is tried, it is likely to be ignored. A classic case was when cost-benefit analysis of water resource spending suggested a different formula for the allocation of money. The water resource subgovernment quickly ignored the new formula, which was threatening to the standard way of distributing benefits that had been built up by many supporters and clients over the years (see Ripley and Franklin, 1984: 115).

On the other hand, where visibility and level of controversy are higher, where duration is longer, and where the number of actors is greater, there is a much larger chance that analysts will be at work and that they will make recommendations relevant to the policy area. However, although the conditions here allow and even encourage more analysis (with some of the contending parties promoting what they hope will be analyses supporting their views—although good analysts will surely resist the effort to become "hired guns"), the same conditions also make it likely that analysis will play only a small role in the final outcome. All kinds of political forces are at play in such decision making, and analysis cannot bulk very large most of the time in such a setting. Thus, decisions about protective regulation, redistribution, and strategic policy invite analysis but discourage its use or at least put it in the position of a relatively weak competitor for attention.

Analysis in crisis situations is, by definition, prohibited because of the shortness of time, although there could be anticipatory analysis of decision making in crises in general. Analysis in competitive regulatory policy tends to be short-run and decision specific because of the nature of what gets done in that arena.

The Impact of Research Support on Policy Analysis

Most policy analysis takes place under the sponsorship of governmental units that find such analysis directly useful. There is some "in-house" policy analysis of various kinds conducted by individual federal agencies, central executive branch agencies, a few national commissions, committees of Congress, and especially some of the central staff agencies of

Congress such as the General Accounting Office, the Congressional Budget Office, and the Office of Technology Assessment. Most policy analysis outside the government is sponsored by the bureaucratic agencies directly concerned. A little is also supported by a few national commissions. Additional policy analysis—again, very limited in amount—is supported by private foundations in areas of policy important to them.

"In-house" policy analysis is, by definition, totally dependent on decisions by units of the government about how much analysis they want, why they want it, when they want it, and what they want evaluated and analyzed. By definition, the objectivity of such analysis has to be suspect. It could be objective, but there are powerful reasons to assume that any individual agency is pursuing some policy preferences when it settles on any specific line of internal research.

Policy research done outside the government is almost totally dependent on funding from the government, in this case almost always the agencies responsible for individual programs. A little policy research money for outsiders comes from a few national commissions. A few government agencies sponsoring "basic" research (as opposed to presumed "applied" research), such as the National Science Foundation, support a few policy-relevant studies. And a few private foundations support some studies.

There is, of course, nothing automatically "objective" about policy analysis done outside the government by either academics or in private research companies. Those funding such research no doubt have a policy agenda. Outsiders who agree to do policy research on grant or contract (even with a private foundation) may well be swayed in how they approach their work by those agendas. At minimum, the choice of what to study is in part dependent on those agencies. Outsiders, especially those in universities, presumably negotiate the right to data, the right to publication, and—at absolute minimum—the right to arrive at any findings supported by the data, but there is no fixed pattern for the outcomes of such negotiations. Different agencies and researchers have very different traditions about the conditions under which policy analysis goes forward. In the final section of this chapter, I will discuss what I have termed "the clinical relationship" as one way of subsuming a lot of questions about the relationship between sponsor and researcher, including questions that bear on "objectivity." Needless to say, there is no way to guarantee "objectivity" since it is unclear what it means. More important, bias of various sorts may be introduced either by the sponsor, by the researcher, and by an interaction between them, and not all bias is based on conscious choices.

The general pressure of the funding sources for policy analysis in the last few decades has been to view virtually all policy analysis as "applied" and not "basic" research (for a good summary of the developments only briefly referred to in the next few paragraphs, see Social Science Research Council, 1983). The two principal developments that made it inevitable that most policy analysis would be funded by the "action agencies" directly responsible for individual programs can be summarized simply. First, foundations, which had provided almost all funding for social science research before World War II, began after the war to shift their priorities from basic to applied research. Marshall Robinson, writing in a Social Science Research Council symposium (1983:38), offers a good summary:

"One of the important changes in the foundations' role in the support of social research stems from a growing conviction among foundation leaders that social scientists should be viewed primarily as instruments for dealing with complex social issues. Unlike the situation in the 1920s, 1930s, and 1950s, when the foundations' support was largely for basic research, foundation attention in the past two decades has increasingly focused on problem solving. Thus, by 1964 the leading foundations were providing roughly equal amounts for basic and applied research, and by 1980 basic research was getting less than a quarter of the total—and a large share of that basic research support was from a single source and for a single discipline: the Sloan Foundation, for the support of economics."

Second, the National Science Foundation, when created after World War II, was enjoined by Congress to deal with basic rather than applied research. As the social sciences became a legitimate subject for funding in the years following the founding of NSF, this mandate continued. NSF defined policy analysis as applied. A few add-on programs in the last few years have allowed some policy analysis to take place with NSF support, but not much.

In general, political science is not one of the heavily funded social sciences when the entire federal spending on social sciences (both "basic" and "applied") is considered. In the period between 1967 and 1983, for example, only 3.8 percent of the research spending of all federal agencies on social sciences went to political science (the only other three disciplines designated as social sciences in this comparison were anthropology, economics, and sociology). NSF spent 11.8 percent of its money for these four social sciences on political science. Both figures put political science at the bottom of these four disciplines, in relative terms. Total funding for social sciences from the federal government in 1980 has been estimated at $524 million. That figure has shrunk in the Reagan years (see Consortium of Social Science Associations, 1983).

Another compilation of recent spending (National Science Foundation, 1983) shows that all federal obligations for both basic and applied research to political science were very small both in absolute numbers and when compared to four other social sciences on which data are reported (psychology, anthropology, economics, and sociology). Even in absolute dollars the growth in political science in the period from 1975 to 1984 was tiny. When inflation is taken into account, of course, federal support actually shrank. None of the social sciences is well funded in terms of federal support. But political science is clearly the weakest of the five in absolute terms and one of the weakest in terms of a pattern of no net growth over the past decade. Table 7.1 summarizes federal support to these five social sciences in Fiscal Year 1975, Fiscal Year 1979 (the high point for political science in absolute dollars over the last decade), and Fiscal Year 1984 (the last year of data included in the NSF report). The table shows low absolute dollars for political science, a small pattern of growth in dollars not corrected for inflation in the decade between 1975 and 1984, and the largest shrinkage between a relatively good year (in 1979) and 1984.

The Clinical Relationship

The central argument of this section can be stated simply:

1. Social scientists can simultaneously learn from and contribute to the makers and implementers of public policy in the course of conducting and reporting empirical research.

2. "Learn from" means that social scientists can advance knowledge in their own disciplines.

3. "Contribute to" means that various aspects of the policy process and the substance of policy can be changed (presumably for the better) because policy makers and implementers can acquire useful diagnoses and prescriptions from social scientists.

4. The relationship that allows the simultaneous learning and contributing for social scientists can be described best as "clinical." A clinical relationship allows both disciplinary values and values of the decision makers to be served by the same research.

Much discussion of the potential role of political science specifically has been included in some of the foregoing chapters. To conclude this book, I will refer to social science generically to indicate the important commonalities political science has with other social science disciplines that also contain policy analysis interests and specialists.

Table 7.1

Federal Obligations to Selected Social Sciences for All Basic and Applied Research, Fiscal Years 1975, 1979, and 1984

Discipline	Fiscal Years (Millions of Dollars)			Percent Change	
	FY 75	FY 79	FY 84(est.)	FY 75 to FY 84	FY 79 to FY 84
Psychology	54.8	89.8	98.3	+79	+ 9
Economics	33.5	45.6	52.6	+57	+15
Sociology	12.8	24.2	23.9	+87	− 1
Anthropology	6.3	7.8	7.1	+13	− 9
Political Science	2.4	5.2	2.8	+17	−46

Source: National Science Foundation (1983) *Federal Funds for Research and Development: Detailed Historical Tables: Fiscal Years 1955–1984*, pp. 404–7.

The Meaning of a Clinical Relationship

The word *clinical* has been chosen to describe a special relationship between social scientists (especially those based in universities) and public decision makers. Since the word is used here in a new context, its meaning is discussed with some care. Several dictionary definitions have partial relevance. The *Unabridged Random House Dictionary of the English Language* defines clinical as "concerned with or based on actual observation and treatment of disease in patients rather than artificial experimentation or theory," and as "extremely objective and realistic." A clinic is defined as "any class or group convening for instruction, remedial work, etc., in a special field." The *American Heritage Dictionary of the English Language* defines clinical as "analytical; highly objective; rigorously scientific," and defines a clinic as "a center that offers counsel or instruction."

When these definitions are aggregated, some of the principal meanings I intend are captured. First, a clinical relationship involves at least two parties and is a joint venture (I would argue that a healthy teacher-student, counselor-counselee, or doctor-patient relationship is a two-way relationship and that both parties learn as well as teach, frequently reversing formal roles). Second, a clinical relationship partakes of the scientific spirit, which includes a striving for objectivity, realism, and analytical rigor. Third, the learning and teaching that occur in a clinical relationship are based on empirical observation. Fourth, the explicit point of the relationship is to solve practical problems in the short-run and to establish the basis for good theory that can be used in the future.

The medical origins of the word need not be a hindrance (*empirical* also has a medical meaning). I certainly do not intend any foolish and rigid medical analogy. Even in present ordinary usage, however, the word *clinical* is not limited to its medical meaning (as some of the above dictionary definitions make clear). Certainly, "disease" on the part of decision makers or their institutions need not be assumed, nor are decision makers "patients" in the classic sense. To realize that decision makers have problems that need solutions and that they can work with social scientists to achieve some partial solutions to those problems, however, is not farfetched. Even in the strictly medical clinical relationship, there is payoff for both parties. The potential payoff for the patient is that problems are identified and treated, and the goal of better health is achieved. The potential payoff for the doctor is that he or she will learn by observation so that diagnostic and prescriptive powers are enhanced and better focused for use with subsequent patients. In short, a skillful doctor builds or extends theory that can be applied subsequently.

The point of my using a familiar word in a new sense is that no other word quite captures the meaning I intend. "Consultative" implies an exclusive focus on short-range problems and a one-way flow of expertise. Compound forms of policy or policy analysis (such as policy-relevant) used to describe the relationship are too vague and amorphous in view of the vast array of enterprises that are identified or self-identified as being in that mold.

The Notion of Clinical Utility

Social science research that is clinically useful is perceived by decision makers faced with concrete choices among policy and program alternatives (choices that almost certainly have to be made within specific time constraints) to have direct and immediate payoff in terms of making "better" choices. From the point of view of the researcher, clinically useful research involves harnessing new or existing knowledge to a concrete problem or set of problems recognized or acknowledged by decision makers. The clinically oriented researcher and the relevant decision makers should work together in a partnership to define the problem and the perceived problem-solving needs. Then, the research design must address that problem and those needs in explicit terms.

Advice that will convey clear messages to decision makers should state conclusions fully and clearly. This means that clinically useful research must be evaluative in a number of significant ways. Judgments about "more productive" versus "less productive" alternatives, or about "better" versus "worse" alternatives, should be stated by the researchers with reference to a range of phenomena— past and projected—so that such judgments may be perceived by the decision makers.

This does not mean, however, that the clinically oriented social scientists who perforce become evaluators (that is, who make explicit qualitative judgments based on their research) need to operate from only a single goal perspective, whether it be their own or someone else's that they adopt. Indeed, the most useful work is likely to be reported in terms of several different goal perspectives, some of which may be quite incompatible with each other. One reason this way of proceeding is more likely to be useful to decision makers is that they continually face pressures that have embedded in them differing and often conflicting goals. If a researcher can present findings coupled with an articulation of where different perspectives lead and how different perspectives might be served best, such a presentation is likely to help clarify choices decision makers will have to make. Such work will not strike them as abstract pieces of research and reasoning without discernible immediate "real world" ties. A second reason for use of multiple goal perspectives is that the researcher may be able to expand the horizons of the decision makers by posing alternative goals not usually pondered.

Two goal perspectives that the researcher-evaluator-clinician might start with are his or her own and that of the decision maker, to the extent that it can be made explicit. A broad range of alternatives should also be considered, if not systematically, at least speculatively. For example, the goal perspective of the clients or intended beneficiaries of a policy or program is often not articulated clearly, if at all, by decision makers. Researchers can perform a potential service by providing such articulation and by linking it to empirical analysis of past performance or to empirically supported forecasting of alternative futures. The goal perspectives of leading competing interest groups might also be articulated, even though the decision maker may be partially aware of them because of perceived pressures. There might also be a broad societal perspective (national interest, public good) that can be given some concrete meaning by a careful researcher presenting his or her findings to decision makers.

General Conditions for Clinically Useful Social Science Research

Several writers have given attention to the question of how to structure research so that it has at least a good chance of being useful. The most general point that often emerges is that the research design must be developed in order to fit the purposes of the policy research. Various kinds of designs—experimental, statistical, comparative case studies—may be appropriate or inappropriate, depending on specific purposes (see Van Meter and Van Horn, 1975b). Variables must be consciously chosen for policy purposes (Brewer, 1973), and some of the critical ones must be manipulable or actionable by policy makers.

Another condition seems useful to explore: that the research should be designed not just with variables, hypotheses, and so on, appropriate for policy research but with a specific client or a class of clients in mind. A design for clinically useful policy research must meet requirements over and above the rigorous methodology and theoretical promise demanded of all "good" science. By the very fact that it is policy research, it is expected to address issues of substantive and proximate importance in society. Few characterizing themselves as policy analysts would object to that requirement. Yet, there is disagreement over whether or not research should or should not be designed for specific clients.

There is no need to argue that all research on policy has to be designed for specific clients or classes of clients to make the point that if research is to be perceived as clinically useful by those for whom it is intended, the chances for such perceptions to emerge are greatly enhanced if the original design is undertaken with them in mind and especially in consultation with them. At minimum, the design of policy-relevant research should not preclude its being perceived as clinically useful. But I would argue that the odds are against utilization of policy research unless the original design and major modifications in it are undertaken for specific clients, ideally in meaningful consultation with them (see Lyons, 1975, on the importance of such consultation). Clinical utility requires that problems for research be defined in part on the basis of problems perceived by prospective clients. Variables and findings, moreover, must be stated in terms compatible with clients' perceptions of problems.

A number of legitimate doubts have been expressed by some social scientists about the legitimacy of the social scientist acting as a clinician. These range from concern with the impositions of security to concern about the propriety of accepting politically defined issues as research topics. Horowitz (1970:340) states the problem in general: "Social scientists engaged in governmental work are committed to an advocacy model defined by politicians. For the most part, they do not establish or even verify policy—only legitimize policy. They are, in effect, the great mandarins of the present era. They proclaim a position, more than prove its efficacy or necessity. They operate within a teleological model rather than a causal model. They enter at the termination, not the beginning of the policy-making process."

The Horowitz position can be contradicted in a number of ways, although, at root, some ideological disagreements between Horowitz and those more clinically minded are likely never to be settled (and there is no reason to insist that they should be). One way to answer Horowitz is empirically—that is, by striving to involve social scientists at the stage of intelligence (near the beginning of the policy-making process) as well as at the stage of appraisal or evaluation (see Lasswell, 1971). If Horowitz is demanding that social scientists somehow set or dominate policies in relation to which they do research, he is writing social scientists out of the possibility of doing anything that is deliberately relevant to policy makers. To that position there is no answer save a counterclaim that society is likely to be ill-advised to give many of its resources to a social science so intent on isolating itself from people who make decisions for society.

Many of the obstructions to the practical application of social science research efforts derive not from the unwillingness of scholars to provide information to the practitioner nor even from the latter's unwillingness to be informed, but rather from the wide divergence in orientation and procedure of the two—a divergence manifested merely by the difference between the kinds of information desired and the sort provided. The scientist seeks understanding, whereas the policy maker seeks a guide to action. Hence, the former treats data with a view to explanation, while the latter wants the data to serve as a basis for formulating and implementing decisions (Riecken, 1969:1; Horowitz, 1970:354). The scientist is abstract and treats the particular primarily in order to generalize from it; the practitioner is particularistic and concrete, tolerating generalization only to the extent that it is useful in guiding action in a specific case. The result is neatly described by Polk (1965:243), who proposes that "the question the 'operator' wants answered is on the order of 'Will they rumble at four o'clock on 97th Street?' " The social scientists' typical response is likely to be concerned with the question: "What forces in society cause young men and women in urban society to rumble?"

The social scientist serving as a clinician can expect the greatest success in developing an attentive audience of key policy makers if he or she focuses on some aspects of the intelligence and appraisal functions, broadly defined. Within the intelligence function, policy makers are likely to be most receptive to the provision of descriptive trends that relate to the present possibilities of goal achievement. Also, within the intelligence function the clinician might find some responsiveness to efforts to assist with goal clarification.

Within the appraisal function several objects for evaluation can be suggested as the strongest candidates in terms of developing a fruitful clinical relationship. These include policy processes and implementation, as well as programmatic outcomes or impacts. A number of barriers exist to the establishment of successful clinical relationships, of course. I have no desire to catalog them here, but I want to underscore the point that an aspiring clinician can reduce his or her own chances for success by focusing primarily on individual policy formulation and implementation choices (especially those that are highly politicized) on a day-to-day basis and in detail. These activities may be worth doing, but to focus on them to the exclusion of the broader activities just outlined is to foredoom the policy scientist to a life of frustration and self-pity. This is not to imply that dealing with the intelligence and appraisal functions is politically "neutral"—but they do seem to be functions in relation to which the claim of professional expertise can be most soundly based and in which the intricacies of day-to-day politics seem more remote. It may be that much "grander" sets of political choices are being made at the symbolic beginning and ending points of intelligence and appraisal, but the pressures on policy makers are usually structured so that it seems more legitimate to them to acknowledge and to use social science at these stages rather than in the middle, more detailed stages.

A focus on intelligence and appraisal offers benefits to the policy maker while minimizing the likelihood that threats will also be perceived. The same focus also holds more scientific or disciplinary promise than a focus on the more detailed day-to-day matters in the stages between intelligence and appraisal.

It is clear that the first problem facing a design for policy research is that of bounding the universe of variables to which attention will be directed. It is also the most difficult task for the scientist, for it implies the necessity of establishing those boundaries not only according to traditional considerations of theoretical interest or empirical promise, but also on the basis of user interest and potential manipulability. If the research problem is conceived as a multiple regression equation, it might be that the first several terms account for 80 percent of the variance in the dependent variable. To the scientist interested in explanation, this may be of central interest. But if the variables represented by the terms in question are not susceptible to manipulation by the policy maker or if they are unlikely to vary sufficiently to effect a relatively short-term forecast, then they have a reduced place in the analysis. More attention should focus on the remaining terms—the manipulable variables.

The central condition necessary as a prelude to clinically useful work is a client orientation on the part of the researchers. This same concern also pushes in the direction of identifying institutional structural variables as particularly important for clinically useful research because most policy makers have much more manipulative potential in dealing with such variables than they do in dealing with the "fancier" variables of abstract social science.

Concluding Thoughts about Clinical Utility

The essence of the clinical relationship can be summarized briefly. It is a two-way relationship between outside research analyst and sponsor/client. Both parties teach and learn in the relationship. It needs to be based on mutual trust. Interaction needs to take place at four critical points in the research process:

1. During research design, in order to make sure that the legitimate interests of both the analysts (contributing to broader knowledge based on policy analysis) and the sponsors (a focus on manipulable variables

that allows meaningful recommendations to be made) will be addressed.
2. In connection with planning the timetable of the project, in order to make it feasible for the analysts and also to make it timely in terms of utilizability for the sponsors.
3. During the course of the project, serious joint attention needs to be given by both parties to both written and oral reports. It seems perfectly appropriate to have negotiations over mid-course corrections as one result of such written reports and oral briefings.
4. At the end of the project there needs to be serious interaction over the meaning of the findings and implications and recommendations for action stemming from those findings.

The danger of a clinical relationship is, of course, that the sponsor will simply become a patron and the analyst will become a kept analyst. However, there is reason to believe that an outside analyst can successfully maintain a critical stance with regard to the programs being studied and can also maintain a broader perspective than just the limited one afforded by the program itself. That broader perspective may come from theory or from comparative knowledge of other programs or from both. A critical stance may not be easy to maintain, but without the maintenance of such a stance, much policy analysis necessarily has to be suspect.

If policy research is undertaken with a clinical perspective and under the proper kinds of conditions (consultation and decision-relevant research design), then the alleged "gap" between the worlds of thought and action can be closed a bit. A view of the gap as an unbridgeable chasm is unrealistic unless it is rooted in an ideology that demands the maintenance of a chasm as an article of faith. Bargains will need to be struck between the parties in a clinical relationship, but those bargains can be mutually profitable, and in no way are the parties trapped in a zero-sum situation. Both research and utilization can be improved simultaneously under proper conditions.

At least some social scientists should seek clinical relevance. The reasons for this position are several. First, disciplines that speak only to themselves and do not seek relevance to a wider segment of society—particularly when those disciplines are developing knowledge about socially important phenomena—seem to be courting the unenviable status of reducing their own marginal utility to society so severely that society will, in a variety of ways, stop supporting the enterprise. Survival is not always justified, but it is curious to ponder an entire set of disciplines that would deliberately and willingly jeopardize their survival.

Second, disciplines that study society yet seek to interact with important parts of it only in an arms-length mode cut off communication that can lead, at minimum, to more insightful research designs and better data and, given the differing perspectives as well as numbers of intelligent and thoughtful people in the policy arena, a broader and more fruitful framework for interpreting results.

Third, one does not have to be smug or self-satisfied about the social sciences collectively and individually, or totally skeptical about the state of any kind of policy analysis in almost any policy-relevant institution at any territorial level, to be willing to entertain as plausible the assertion that social scientists working with policy makers (not preaching to them) can help improve the quality of policy analysis. It also seems plausible that such improvement will lead, partially and incrementally, to a more efficient use of social resources in dealing with important problems facing society.

References

Bachrach, Peter, and Morton S. Baratz. "Two Faces of Power." *American Political Science Review* (1962), 56:947–952.

Bailey, Stephen K. *Congress Makes a Law: The Story Behind the Employment Act of 1946.* New York: Columbia University Press, 1950.

Baumer, Donald C., and Carl E. Van Horn. *The Politics of Unemployment.* Washington, D.C.: Congressional Quarterly Press, 1984.

Borus, Michael E. *Measuring the Impact of Employment-Related Social Programs.* Kalamazoo, Mich.: Upjohn Institute, 1979.

Brewer, Garry D. *Politicians, Bureaucrats, and the Consultant.* New York: Basic Books, 1973.

Brewer, Garry D., and Peter deLeon. *The Foundations of Policy Analysis.* Homewood, Ill.: Dorsey, 1983.

Clark, Kenneth B. "Social Policy, Power, and Social Science Research." *Harvard Educational Review* 43 (1973): 113–121.

Cobb, Roger W., and Charles D. Elder. *Participation in American Politics: The Dynamics of Agenda-Building,* 2d ed. Baltimore, Md.: Johns Hopkins University Press, 1983.

Cobb, Roger, Jennie-Keith Ross, and Marc Howard Ross. "Agenda Building as a Comparative Political Process." *American Political Science Review* 70 (1976): 126–138.

Coleman, James S. *Policy Research in the Social Sciences.* Morristown, N.J.: General Learning Press, 1972.

Coleman, James S., Sara D. Kelley, and John H. Moore. *Trends in School Segregation, 1968–1973.* Washington, D.C.: Urban Institute, 1975.

Coleman, James S. et al. *Equality of Educational Opportunity.* Washington, D.C.: U.S. Government Printing Office, 1966.

Committee on Department of Labor Research and Development, Assembly of Behavioral and Social Sciences, National Research Council. *Knowledge and Power in Manpower: A Study of the Manpower Research and Development Program in the Department of Labor.* Washington, D.C.: National Academy of Sciences, 1975.

Consortium of Social Science Associations. *COSSA Washington Update,* vol. 2, no. 23 (Dec. 16, 1983).

Crawford, Elizabeth T., and Albert D. Biderman. "The Functions of Policy-Oriented Social Science." In Crawford and Biderman (eds.), *Social Scientists and International Affairs.* New York: Wiley, 1969.

Crick, Bernard. *The American Science of Politics: Its Origins and Conditions.* Berkeley: University of California Press, 1959.

Dahl, Robert A., and Charles E. Lindblom. *Politics, Economics, and Welfare.* New York: Harper, 1953.

Derthick, Martha. *New Towns In-Town.* Washington, D.C.: Urban Institute, 1972.

Eyestone, Robert. *From Social Issues to Public Policy.* New York: Wiley, 1978.

Franklin, Grace A., and Randall B. Ripley. *CETA: Politics and Policy, 1973–1982.* Knoxville: University of Tennessee Press, 1984.

Froman, Lewis A., Jr. "The Categorization of Policy Contents." In Austin Ranney (ed.), *Political Science and Public Policy.* Chicago, Ill.: Markham, 1968.

Hargrove, Erwin C. "The Bureaucratic Politics of Evaluation: A Case Study of the Department of Labor." *Public Administration Review* 40 (1980): 150–159.

Havelock, R. G. *Planning for Innovation through Dissemination and Utilization of Knowledge.* Ann Arbor, Mich.: Center for Research on Utilization of Scientific Knowledge, 1969.

Hayes, Michael T. *Lobbyists and Legislators: A Theory of Political Markets.* New Brunswick, N.J.: Rutgers University Press, 1981.

Horowitz, Irving L. "Social Science Mandarins: Policymaking as a Practical Formula."*Policy Sciences* 1 (1970): 339–360.

Huntington, Samuel P. *The Common Defense.* New York: Columbia University Press, 1961.

Janowitz, Morris. "Professionalization of Sociology." *American Journal of Sociology* 78 (1972): 105–135.

Jencks, Christopher et al. *Inequality: A Reassessment of the Effect of Family and Schooling in America.* New York: Basic Books, 1972.

Jones, Charles O. "Policy Analysis: Academic Utility for Practical Rhetoric." *Policy Studies Journal* 4 (1976): 281–286.

Jones, Charles O. "American Politics and the Organization of Energy Decision Making." *Annual Review of Energy* 4 (1979): 99–121.

Jones, Charles O. *An Introduction to the Study of Public Policy,* 3d ed. Monterey, Calif.: Brooks/Cole, 1984.

Kaufman, Herbert. *The Forest Ranger.* Baltimore, Md.: Johns Hopkins University Press, 1960.

Kaufman, Herbert. *Administrative Feedback.* Washington, D.C.: Brookings Institution, 1973.

King, Anthony. "Ideas, Institutions and the Policies of Governments: A Comparative Analysis." *British Journal of Political Science* 3 (1973): 291–313; 409–423.

Kingdon, John W. *Agendas, Alternatives, and Public Policies.* Boston, Mass.: Little, Brown, 1984.

Kluger, Richard. *Simple Justice: The History of* Brown v. Board of Education *and Black America's Struggle for Equality.* New York: Knopf, 1976.

Knott, Jack, and Aaron Wildavsky. "If Dissemination Is the Solution, What Is the Problem?" *Knowledge* 1 (1980): 537–578.

Lasswell, Harold D. *A Pre-View of Policy Sciences.* New York: American Elsevier, 1971.

Lerner, Daniel, and Harold D. Lasswell, eds. *The Policy Sciences: Recent Developments in Scope and Methods.* Stanford, Calif.: Stanford University Press, 1951.

Lindblom, Charles E. *The Intelligence of Democracy*. New York: Free Press, 1965.

Lowi, Theodore J. "American Business, Public Policy, Case-Studies, and Political Theory." *World Politics* 16 (1964): 677–715.

Lowi, Theodore J. "Making Democracy Safe for the World: National Politics and Foreign Policy." In James N. Rosenau (ed.), *Domestic Sources of Foreign Policy*. New York: Free Press, 1967.

Lowi, Theodore J. "Four Systems of Policy, Politics, and Choice." *Public Administration Review* 32 (1972): 298–310.

Lowi, Theodore J. "What Political Scientists Don't Need to Ask About Policy Analysis." *Policy Studies Journal* 2 (1973): 61–67.

Lynn, Laurence E., Jr., ed. *Knowledge and Policy: The Uncertain Connection*. Washington, D.C.: National Academy of Sciences, 1978.

Lyons, Gene M., ed. *Social Research and Public Policies*. Hanover, N.H.: Dartmouth College Public Affairs Center, 1975.

Matthews, Donald R. *U.S. Senators and Their World*. Chapel Hill: University of North Carolina Press, 1960.

National Science Foundation. *Federal Funds for Research and Development*, 2 vols. Washington, D.C.: National Science Foundation Division of Science Resources Studies, 1983.

Page, Benjamin I. *Who Gets What from Government*. Berkeley: University of California Press, 1983.

Palumbo, Dennis J. "The State of Policy Studies Research and the Policy of the New *Policy Studies Review*." *Policy Studies Review* 1 (1981): 5–10.

Patton, Michael Q. *Utilization-Focused Evaluation*. Beverly Hills, Calif.: Sage Publications, 1978.

Polk, William R. "Problems of Government Utilization of Scholarly Research in International Affairs." *Background* 9 (1965): 240–245.

Polsby, Nelson W. *Political Innovation in America: The Politics of Policy Initiation*. New Haven, Conn.: Yale University Press, 1984.

Pressman, Jeffrey L., and Aaron Wildavsky. *Implementation*, 2d ed. Berkeley: University of California Press, 1979.

Ranney, Austin, ed. *Political Science and Public Policy*. Chicago, Ill.: Markham, 1968.

Ravitch, Diane. *The Troubled Crusade: American Education, 1945–1980*. New York: Basic Books, 1983.

Riecken, Henry W. "Social Sciences and Contemporary Social Problems." *Social Science Research Council Items* 23 (1969): 1–6.

Ripley, Randall B. *The Politics of Economic and Human Resource Development*. Indianapolis, Ind.: Bobbs-Merrill, 1972.

Ripley, Randall B., and associates. *The Implementation of CETA in Ohio*. Employment and Training Administration R&D Monograph 44. Washington, D.C.: U.S. Government Printing Office, 1977.

Ripley, Randall B., and associates. *CETA Prime Sponsor Management Decisions and Program Goal Achievement*. Employment and Training Administration R&D Monograph 56. Washington, D.C.: U.S. Government Printing Office, 1978.

Ripley, Randall B., and associates. *Areawide Planning in CETA*. Employment and Training Administration R&D Monograph 74. Washington, D.C.: U.S. Government Printing Office, 1979.

Ripley, Randall B., and Grace A. Franklin, eds. *Policy-Making in the Federal Executive Branch*. New York: Free Press, 1975.

Ripley, Randall B., and Grace A. Franklin. *Bureaucracy and Policy Implementation*. Homewood, Ill.: Dorsey, 1982.

Ripley, Randall B., and Grace A. Franklin. *Congress, the Bureaucracy, and Public Policy*, 3rd ed. Homewood, Ill.: Dorsey, 1984.

Ripley, Randall B., and Lance M. Smith. "The Implementation of HIRE II: Final Report." In Committee on Veterans' Affairs, *Oversight of Veterans' Employment Programs and Policies*, Hearing before Committee on Veterans' Affairs, United States Senate, May 12, 1979, pp. 720–797.

Rosenau, James N. "Moral Fervor, Systematic Analysis, and Scientific Consciousness in Foreign Policy Research." In Austin Ranney (ed.), *Political Science and Public Policy*. Chicago, Ill.: Markham, 1968.

Rosenthal, Alan, and Carl Van Horn. "The Impact of State Legislative Oversight: a Framework for Analysis." Paper prepared for the meeting of the American Political Science Association, Sept. 1982.

Salisbury, Robert H. "The Analysis of Public Policy: A Search for Theories and Roles." In Austin Ranney (ed.), *Political Science and Public Policy*. Chicago, Ill.: Markham, 1968.

Social Science Research Council. "Research Support and Intellectual Advance in the Social Sciences: A Symposium." *Items* 37 (1983): 33–49.

Somit, Albert, and Joseph Tanenhaus. *The Development of American Political Science: From Burgess to Behavioralism*. Boston, Mass.: Allyn and Bacon, 1967.

Van Horn, Carl E. *Policy Implementation in the Federal System: National Goals and Local Implementors*. Lexington, Mass.: D. C. Heath, 1979.

Van Horn, Carl E., and Donald S. Van Meter. "The Implementation of Intergovernmental Policy." In Charles O. Jones and Robert D. Thomas (eds.), *Public Policy Making in a Federal System*. Beverly Hills, Calif.: Sage Publications, 1976.

Van Meter, Donald S., and Carl E. Van Horn. "The Policy Implementation Process: A Conceptual Framework." *Administration and Society* 6 (1975): 445–487. (a)

Van Meter, Donald S., and Carl E. Van Horn. "Studying Implementation." Paper prepared for the meeting of the American Political Science Association, 1975. (b)

Weiss, Carol H. "The Many Meanings of Research Utilization." *Public Administration Review* 39 (1979): 426–431.

Weiss, Carol H. "Knowledge Creep and Decision Accretion." *Knowledge* 1 (1980): 381–404.

Williams, Walter, et al. *Studying Implementation: Methodological and Administrative Issues*. Chatham, N.J.: Chatham House, 1982.

Wilson, James Q. " 'Policy Intellectuals' and Public Policy." *The Public Interest*, no. 64 (1981): 31–46.

Wright, Richard L. "Research Utilization in Public Policy Making: The Case of the Targeted Jobs Tax Credit." Ph.D. dissertation, Ohio State University, Columbus, 1984.

Index

225